KU-707-944

The Observer's Book of

BUTTERFLIES

Compiled by
W. J. STOKOE

Foreword by
N. D. RILEY, C.B.E., F.R.E.S.
formerly Keeper of the Department of
Entomology, British Museum
(Natural History)

Describing
69 BRITISH SPECIES
with over 150 illustrations in colour
and black and white

FREDERICK WARNE

LONDON

First published 1937 by
Frederick Warne & Co. Ltd
© Frederick Warne & Co. Ltd, London

21st impression 1966
Revised edition 1969
Fourth reprint of revised edition 1977

© Fifth reprint (with some additional revisions) 1979

ISBN 0 7232 1519 7

Printed & bound in Great Britain by
William Clowes (Beccles) Limited
Beccles and London
D5943.579

FOREWORD

It might well be asked whether yet another book on the British butterflies is necessary; whether indeed it would not be better to try and screen from inquisitive eyes and hide from grasping hands those butterflies that still remain to us. That is not possible. The only course that lies open to us is that which leads through education to a proper appreciation of nature as a subject, not for wanton, thoughtless destruction, but for careful preservation and study, to be treasured for the joy it can bring to the seeing eye and the thoughtful mind.

In these days of quick and easy transport the countryside is no longer the sanctuary it was for nature, and unless we are careful, those who come after us may justly accuse us of betraying the trust we hold for them.

Such a book as this, therefore, complete in itself, accurate, reliable and convenient to use, is one of the best safeguards that can be provided, since it leaves no grounds for a plea of ignorance where our butterflies are concerned.

N. D. R.

PREFACE

All the coloured illustrations have been reproduced from accurate drawings by H. D. Swain, and the black and white figures are by Mr. Horace Knight. They are all of natural size, except the eggs, which are shown as very much enlarged. Coloured illustrations marked "U" indicate under wing colouring. In some cases both male (♂) and female (♀) wings are shown.

The descriptions of the species are necessarily confined to the limited space available and technical terms have been avoided as far as possible. They will, however, be found to contain all that is essential for the species to be easily recognized by the observer during a walk in the open country.

CONTENTS

INTRODUCTION

Butterflies belong to the great order of insects called Lepidoptera (Greek *lepis*, a scale, and *pteron*, a wing), that is, insects whose wings are covered with minute structures termed scales.

Moths (Heterocera) also belong to the same order, and the first point to deal with is how may butterflies be distinguished from moths? In a broad kind of way they may be recognized by their feelers (*antennae*), which are gradually or abruptly clubbed at the extremity. For this reason they were designated Rhopalocera, or " club-horned," the Heterocera being supposed to have horns of various kinds other than clubbed.

Although this method of separating moths and butterflies does not hold good in dealing with the Lepidoptera of the world, it will be found that British butterflies may be known, as such, by their clubbed feelers. Only the Burnets among British moths have feelers in any way similar, and these are thickened gradually towards the extremity rather than clubbed. Day-flying moths, especially the bright-coloured ones, might easily be mistaken for butterflies, but in all these the feelers will be found not at all butterfly-like.

A few general remarks on variation in butterflies may here be made. All kinds are liable to vary in tint or in the markings, sometimes in both. Such variation may be only trivial and therefore hardly attracting attention, but in a good many kinds variation is often of a very pronounced character, and is then almost certain to obtain notice. Except in a few instances, where the aberration is of an unusual kind, it is possible to observe all the intermediate stages between the ordinary form of a species and its most extreme variety.

In those kinds of butterflies that attain the perfect state twice in the year, the individuals composing the first brood are somewhat different in marking from those of the second brood. Such species as the Large and Small Whites exhibit this kind of variation, which is termed seasonal dimorphism. The males of some species, as for example the Common Blue and the Orange-tip, differ from the females in colour ; this is known as sexual dimorphism. The Silver-washed Fritillary, which has two forms of the female, one brown like the male, the other greenish in colour, is a good example of dimorphism confined to one

sex. Gynandrous specimens, sometimes errone-
ously called " Hermaphrodites," are those which
exhibit both male and female characters of any
kind in a single individual ; such freaks are
extremely rare.

The ornamentation on the under side of a
butterfly differs from that of the upper side, and
is found to assimilate or harmonize in a remarkable manner with the usual resting-place. It is
therefore of service to the insect when settled
with wings erect over the back, in the manner
adopted by all butterflies, except a few kinds of
Skippers.

The number of known species of butterflies
throughout the world has been put at about
thirteen thousand, and it has been suggested
that there may be several thousand still awaiting
discovery. A list of over seven hundred kinds
of butterflies is catalogued as occurring in the
whole of the Palaearctic Region. This zoo-
logical region embraces Europe, including the
British Islands, Africa north of the Atlas range
of mountains, and temperate Asia, including
Japan. The number of species that can be
regarded as British does not exceed sixty-nine.
Even this limited total comprises sundry migratory butterflies, such as the Clouded Yellows, the
Painted Lady, the Red Admiral, the Camberwell

Beauty, and the Milkweed butterfly; and also the still less frequent, or perhaps more accidental visitors, the Long-tailed Blue and the Bath White. Again, the Large Copper and the Black-veined White are now extinct in England, and the Mazarine Blue does not seem to have been observed in any of its old haunts in this country for very many years.

The majority of the remaining butterflies may be considered natives, and of these about half are so widely distributed that the naturalist should, if fairly energetic, find nearly all of them during his first campaign. The other species will have to be looked for in their special localities, but a few kinds are so strictly attached to particular spots that a good deal of patience will have to be exercised before a chance may occur of finding them.

THE LIFE CYCLE OF A BUTTERFLY

Butterflies pass through three very distinct stages before they attain the perfect form. These stages are: 1. The egg (*ovum*, plural *ova*). 2. The caterpillar (*larva*, *larvae*). 3. The chrysalis (*pupa*, *pupae*). The perfect insect is called the *imago* (plural *imagines*).

THE EGG

Butterfly eggs are of various forms, and whilst in some kinds the egg-shell is elaborately ribbed and fluted, others are simply pitted or covered with a kind of network or reticulation; others, again, are almost or quite smooth. If the top of an egg is examined under a good lens, a depression will be noted, in the middle of which are minute apertures known as micropyles (little doors), and it is through these that the spermatozoa of the male find entry to the interior of the egg and fertilization is effected.

THE CATERPILLAR

The second stage is that of the caterpillar, and in some species this is of very short duration, a few weeks only, whilst in others, it usually lasts for many months. There is considerable diversity both in shape and, where it is present, in the hairy or spiny clothing (*armature*) of caterpillars. All, however, are alike in one respect, that is the body is divided into thirteen more or less well-defined rings (*segments*), which together with the head make up fourteen divisions. The first three nearest the head, each of which is furnished with a pair of true legs (*thoracic legs*), are called the thoracic segments, as they correspond to the thorax of the perfect butterfly. The remaining ten rings are the abdominal segments; the last two are not always easily separable one from the other, and so for all practical purposes they may be considered only nine in number. These nine rings, then, correspond to the abdomen of the future butterfly. The third to sixth of this series have each a pair of false legs (*prolegs*), and there is also a pair on the last ring; the latter are the anal claspers.

The warts (*tubercles*) are the bases of hairs and spines, and are to be seen in most butterfly caterpillars, but they generally require a lens to bring them clearly into view. These warts are usually arranged in two rows on the back (*dorsal series*) and three rows on each side (*lateral series*). All the various parts referred to may be seen in Fig. 1, which also shows a peculiarity that is found in very young caterpillars of the Orange-tip, and in some others of the " Whites." The odd thing about this baby caterpillar is that the fine hair arising from each wart is forked at the tip (Fig. 1, *a*), and holds thereon a minute

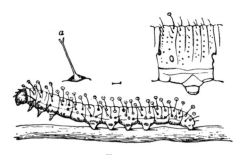

FIG. 1

Young caterpillar of Orange-tip highly magnified.
(*After Sharp*)

globule of fluid. When the caterpillars become about half grown these forked hairs are lost in a general clothing of fine hair. Fig. 1, *b*, represents a magnified single ring of the caterpillar, and this shows a spiracle and the folds of the skin (*subsegments*).

On each ring, except the second, the third, and

14

the last, there is an oval or roundish mark which indicates the position of the breathing hole (*spiracle*). Through these minute openings air enters to the breathing tubes (*tracheae*), which are spread throughout the interior of the caterpillar in a complicated network of main branches and finer twigs ; air is thus conveyed to every part of the body. If one or two air holes become obstructed in any way the caterpillar would possibly be none the worse ; but if all the openings were closed up effectually it would almost certainly die. Total immersion in water, even for some hours, is not always fatal.

a *b*

FIG. 2

(*a*) True and (*b*) false legs.

Referring again to the "feet" of the caterpillar, it will be seen at Fig. 2 that the true legs (*a*) differ from the false legs (*b*) in structure. The former are horny, jointed, and have terminal claws ; the latter are fleshy, with sliding joints, and the foot is furnished with a series of minute hooks (termed crochets) which enable the caterpillar to obtain a secure hold when feeding. The false legs are also the chief means of locomotion, as the true legs are of little service for this purpose. The true legs, however, appear to be of use when the caterpillar is feeding, as the leaf is held between them so as to keep it steady whilst the jaws are doing their work.

Fig. 3 represents the head of a caterpillar, much enlarged, with the mouth parts clearly shown. The biting jaws (*mandibles*) are slightly apart, above them is seen the upper lip (*labrum*), and below them is the under lip (*labium*). The *maxillae* are very tiny affairs, but they should be noted because in the butterfly they become the basal portions of the two tubes which, when united together, form the sucking organ

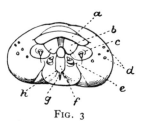

FIG. 3

a, labrum ; *b*, mandible ; *c*, antenna ; *d*, ocelli ; *e*, maxilla ; *f*, labium ; *g*, spinneret ; *h*, labial palp.

(*proboscis*). The eyes, or ocelli as they are termed, are minute, and are said to be of slight use to the caterpillar as organs of sight, so that it probably has to depend on its little feelers (*antennae*) for guidance to the right plants for its nourishment. The spinneret is the organ by means of which the silken threads for its various requirements are provided, the substance itself being secreted in glands placed in the body of the caterpillar. The palpi are organs of touch, and seem to be of use to the caterpillar when moving about.

Immediately after hatching, many caterpillars eat the egg-shell for their first meal; they then settle down to the business of feeding and growing. In the course of a day or two the necessity arises for fasting, as moulting is about to take place. Having spun a slender carpet of silk on a leaf or twig, the caterpillar secures itself thereto, and then awaits the moment for the transformation to commence. After a series of twistings and other contortions, the skin yields along the back near the head, the head is drawn away from its old covering and thrust through the slit in the back, the old skin then peels downwards, whilst the caterpillar draws itself upwards until it is free. The new skin, together with any hairs or spines, is at first very soft. It soon hardens and in a short time all is perfected, and the caterpillar is ready to enter upon its second stage of growth. At the end of the second stage the skin-changing operation is again performed, and the whole business is repeated two or more times afterwards. Finally, however, when the caterpillar has shed its skin for the last time, the chrysalis is revealed, but with the future wings seemingly free. These, together with the other organs, are soon fixed down to the body by the shell, which results from a varnish-like ooze which covers all the parts and then hardens.

Generally speaking, newly hatched caterpillars, though of different kinds, are in certain respects, somewhat alike, but the special characters of each begin to appear, as a rule, after the first change of skin (*ecdysis*), and these go on developing with each successive stage (*stadium*) until the caterpillar is full grown.

THE CHRYSALIS

The scientific term for the chrysalis is *pupa*, which in the Latin tongue means "a doll or puppet."

In passing to the chrysalis stage the caterpillars have sometimes to make rather more preparations than in previous skin-changing provisions. Those of the Swallow-tail, Whites, Orange-tip, and similar kinds have to provide a silken girdle for the waist as well as a pad for the tail. Chrysalids that are suspended, head downwards, such as the Tortoiseshells and Fritillaries, are attached by the cremaster—a hooked arrangement on the tail (Fig. 4)—to a pad of silk; others, such as the Blues and Coppers, appear to be held in position on a leaf, or some other object, by means of a fine girdle of silk, or sometimes a few silken threads spread net-like above and below them. Chrysalids of the Skippers are enclosed in a more or less complete cocoon placed within a chamber, formed of a leaf or leaves of the food-plant, drawn together by silken cables.

A few general remarks on the structure of a chrysalis may be made.

If the upper (*dorsal*) surface of a chrysalis is

examined, the thorax and the body divisions will easily be made out, while, by looking at the sides and the under (*ventral*) surface, the various organs, such as the wings, legs, antennae, etc., will be found neatly laid along each side of the " tongue "

FIG. 4

Enlarged view of cremaster, and a hook still more enlarged. (*After Sharp*)

or proboscis, which latter extends down the centre. All these are separately encased, although they appear to be welded together.

When the butterfly is ready to emerge, the shell of the chrysalis splits along the thorax and at the lower end of the wing-cases, and the insect is then able to release itself from the pupal trappings. The manner of the breaking open of the chrysalis shell varies in different species.

The emergence of a butterfly from the chrysalis is always a most interesting operation to observe, and everyone should make a point of watching the process, so that practical knowledge may be obtained of how the thing is done.

THE BUTTERFLY

Having safely cleared itself free of the chrysalis shell, the butterfly makes its way to some suitable twig, or other object, from which it can hang, usually in an inverted position, whilst a very important function takes place. This is the distention and drying of the wings, which at first are very weak and somewhat baggy, although the colour and markings appear upon them in miniature. All other parts of the butterfly seem fully formed, but the helpless condition of the wings alone prevent it as yet from flying off into the air. In a very short time, after the insect has settled to the business, the fluids from the body commence to flow and circulate through the wings, and these are seen gradually expanding and filling out until they attain their proper size. When the inflation is completed the wings are kept straight out for a time ; they are then motionless, but all their surfaces are well apart. The wings being now fully developed, the further flow of fluid appears to be arrested.

Some of the structural details of the perfect butterfly may now be briefly considered.

When looking at the head of a butterfly (Fig. 5) the first thing to attract the attention is the very large size of the compound eye (*a*). Although so bulky and so complex, the power of sight is not really very keen. A butterfly can see things in a general way readily enough, but it seems unable clearly to distinguish one object from another. When engaged in egg-laying, the female butterfly rarely fails to place her eggs on a leaf or spray of the plant that the future caterpillar will feed upon, and in making this unerring selection, it is suggested that the insect is guided more by the sense of smell than by that of sight.

FIG. 5
Head of Butterfly.
a, compound eye; *b*, palp; *c*, antenna; *d*, proboscis.

The feelers (*antennae*, *c*), which adorn the head, are now considered to be organs of smell. These are composed of a number of segments or rings, which vary in the different kinds of butterfly, as also does the shape of the terminal rings forming what is known as the club. Of the various mouth parts it will only be necessary to refer to the suction-tube, the *proboscis* (*d*), often called the " tongue," which is perhaps the most important, at least to the butterfly itself, as this organ is, in a way, as useful to it in the perfect state as were the strong biting jaws of its caterpillar existence. When not engaged in probing the nectaries of flowers for the sweets they contain, the suction-tube is neatly coiled up between the palpi (*b*). Its great flexibility is due to the many rings of which it is composed. Although seemingly entire, it is really made up of two tubes, each being grooved on its inner side, and forming, when the edges are brought together, an additional central canal, through which the sweets from the flowers are drawn up into a bulb-like receptacle in the head, whence they pass into the stomach. When it is remembered that the passage of sticky fluid through the central tube would most probably result in it becoming clogged, there is reason to suppose that the method of construction permits of the canal being cleansed from time to time.

Reverting to the antennae of butterflies Fig. 6 represents various forms of the club : *e* (Purple Emperor) and *f* (Marbled White) show the gradually thickened club ; in *g* (Brimstone) and *h* (Dark Green Fritillary) the clubs are more or less abruptly formed. Our Skippers have well-developed clubs; these may be hooked at the tip as in *i* (Large Skipper), or blunt at the tip as in *j* (Chequered Skipper).

The important divisions of the body are the thorax and the abdomen. The former is made up of three segments, named pro-thorax, meso-

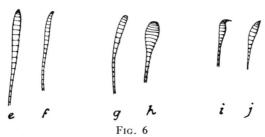

FIG. 6

Antennae of Butterflies.

thorax, and meta-thorax, each of which is furnished with a pair of legs; the second and third segments each bear a pair of wings also. The legs, which in the butterfly are adapted for walking at a leisurely pace, are made up of four main parts; Fig. 7 (*a*) the basal joint (*coxa*), (*b*) the thigh (*femur*), (*c*) the shank (*tibia*), and (*d*) the foot (*tarsus*). The small joint uniting the coxa with the femur is the trochanter (*tr.*). The foot

usually has five joints, the last of which is provided with claws (*e*).

The abdomen really consists of ten rings or
segments. Examined from above, the female
butterfly appears to have only seven rings, and
the male butterfly eight. This discrepancy
arises from the fact that in
the female two rings and in
the male one ring are withdrawn into the body, and
so are tucked away out of
sight. The organs of re-
production are placed in
the terminal ring. The
breathing arrangements are
pretty much as in the caterpillar, but the external
openings are not so ap-
parent owing to the dense
clothing of the body.

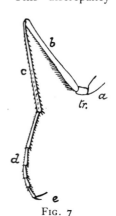

FIG. 7

Leg of Butterfly.

A butterfly's wing con-
sists of an upper and a
lower membrane, with a framework of hollow
tubes, acting as ribs, between the two layers.
Fig. 8, A, shows a fore and hind wing of the
Swallow-tail butterfly. The point of attach-
ment with the thorax is the base of the wing, and
the edge farthest from the base is the outer

margin (*termen*); the upper edge, or front margin, is the *costa*; the lower edge is the inner margin (*dorsum*). The point where the upper margin meets the outer margin on the fore wing is the apex, but on the hind wing it is called the

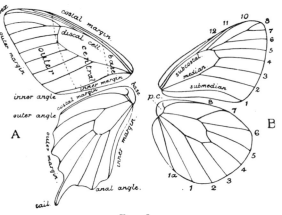

FIG. 8

Butterflies' Wings.

outer angle; the angle formed by the junction of outer and inner margins is the inner angle of the fore wing, and the anal angle of the hind wing. Dividing the wings transversely into three portions, we have three areas, termed basal, central or discal, and outer. These are

25

terms used in descriptions of butterflies, and it
will be useful to remember them.

The ribs of a butterfly's wings are described
as veins, or the main ones nervures, and the
branches nervules.   Fig. 8, B, represents the
venation of the Black-veined White.   Com-
paring the venation of A and B, it will be seen
that in A the fore wing has 12 veins and the hind
wing 8 veins, whilst in B there are only 11 veins
on the fore wing, but the hind wing has one vein
more than that of A.   In the Black-veined
White, vein 9 is absent on the fore wing, and on
the hind wing there is one internal vein (1a).

The beauty of a butterfly's wing is intimately
connected with the form and colour of the scales
with which they are covered, as with a kind of
mosaic.   Dust-like as they appear to the naked
eye, the scales from a butterfly's wing seen under
the microscope are found to be exceedingly
interesting structures and very varied in shape.
They are described as " delicate chitinous bags."
Chitin is the horny substance of which the hard
parts of all insects are made.   As seen on the
wings, the scales are flattened and the upper and
under sides are then almost, or quite, brought
together.   They are attached in lines on the
wing by short stalks which fit into sockets in the
membrane.   The arrangement of the scales,

which has often been stated to resemble that of
the slates on a roof, is shown in Fig. 9.

Colour is chiefly due to pigment contained in
the scale or adhering to the interior of its upper
side. Pigments are stated to be derived, by
various chemical processes, from the blood
while the butterfly is still in the chrysalis stage.

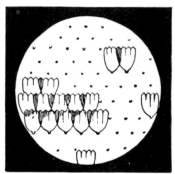

FIG. 9
Arrangement of Scales.
(*After Holland*)

Some scales have minute parallel lines (*striae*)
on their upper sides, and rays of light falling on
these are turned aside or broken up, and so
produce changes in the colouring of a wing
according to the angle from which it is looked at.

The males of many kinds of butterfly have

special scales on the fore wings, which are known as androconia, or plumules. It is believed that these are scent organs. Whatever their particular use may be to the possessor, these androconia enable the entomologist to distinguish male specimens from females with great certainty.

In the foregoing sketch of the life cycle of a butterfly, the object has been to condense as much necessary information as possible into a limited space. Many matters of importance to the student have not been dealt with, but as these are more especially connected with a higher scientific study of the subject than the scope of this little book would allow, they have, therefore, been omitted.

A CODE FOR INSECT COLLECTING

Reprinted by permission of the
JOINT COMMITTEE FOR THE CONSERVATION
OF BRITISH INSECTS

c/o Royal Entomological Society of London,
41 Queens Gate, London, SW7 5HU

This Committee believes that with the ever-increasing loss of habitats resulting from forestry, agriculture, and industrial, urban and recreational development, the point has been reached where a code for collecting should be considered in the interests of conservation of the British insect fauna, particularly macrolepidoptera. The Committee considers that in many areas this loss has gone so far that collecting, which at one time would have had a trivial effect, could now affect the survival in them of one or more species if continued without restraint.

The Committee also believes that by subscribing to a code of collecting, entomologists will show themselves to be a concerned and responsible body of naturalists who have a positive contribution to make to the cause of conservation. It asks all entomologists to accept the following Code in principle and to try to observe it in practice.

1. Collecting—General

1.1 No more specimens than are strictly required for any purpose should be killed.

1.2 Readily identified insects should not be killed if the object is to "look them over" for aberrations or other purposes: insects should be examined while alive and then released where they were captured.

1.3 The same species should not be taken in numbers year after year from the same locality.

1.4 Supposed or actual predators and parasites of insects should not be destroyed.

1.5 When collecting leaf-mines, galls and seed heads never collect all that can be found; leave as many as possible to allow the population to recover.

1.6 Consideration should be given to photography as an alternative to collecting, particularly in the case of butterflies.

1.7 Specimens for exchange, or disposal to other collectors, should be taken sparingly or not at all.

1.8 For commercial purposes insects should be either bred or obtained from old collections.

Insect specimens should not be used for the manufacture of "jewellery".

2. Collecting—rare and endangered species

2.1 Specimens of macrolepidoptera listed by this Committee (and published in the entomological journals) should be collected with the greatest restraint. As a guide, the Committee suggests that a pair of specimens is sufficient, but that those species in the greatest danger should not be collected at all. The list may be amended from time to time if this proves to be necessary.

2.2 Specimens of distinct local forms of Macrolepidoptera, particularly butterflies, should likewise be collected with restraint.

2.3 Collectors should attempt to break new ground rather than collect a local or rare species from a well-known and perhaps over-worked locality.

2.4 Previously unknown localities for rare species should be brought to the attention of this Committee, which undertakes to inform other organizations as appropriate and only in the interests of conservation.

3. Collecting—lights and light-traps

3.1 The " catch " at light, particularly in a trap,

should not be killed casually for subsequent examination.

3.2 Live trapping, for instance in traps filled with egg-tray material, is the preferred method of collecting. Anaesthetics are harmful and should not be used.

3.3 After examination of the catch the insects should be kept in cool, shady conditions and released away from the trap site at dusk. If this is not possible the insects should be released in long grass or other cover and not on lawns or bare surfaces.

3.4 Unwanted insects should not be fed to fish or insectivorous birds and mammals.

3.5 If a trap used for scientific purposes is found to be catching rare or local species unnecessarily it should be re-sited.

3.6 Traps and lights should be sited with care so as not to annoy neighbours or cause confusion.

4. Collecting—permission and conditions

4.1 Always seek permission from landowner or occupier when collecting on private land.

4. Always comply with any conditions laid down by the granting of permission to collect.

4.3 When collecting on nature reserves, or sites of known interest to conservationists, supply a list of species collected to the appropriate authority.

4.4 When collecting on nature reserves it is particularly important to observe the code suggested in section 5.

5. Collecting—damage to the environment

5.1 Do as little damage to the environment as possible. Remember the interests of other naturalists; be careful of nesting birds and vegetation, particularly rare plants.

5.2 When " beating " for lepidopterous larvae or other insects never thrash trees and bushes so that foliage and twigs are removed. A sharp jarring of branches is both less damaging and more effective.

5.3 Coleopterists and others working dead timber should replace removed bark and worked material to the best of their ability. Not all the dead wood in a locality should be worked.

5.4 Overturned stones and logs should be replaced in their original positions.

5.5 Water weed and moss which has been worked for insects should be replaced in its appropriate habitat. Plant material in litter heaps should be replaced and not scattered about.

5.6 Twigs, small branches and foliage required as foodplants or because they are galled, e.g.

by clearwings, should be removed neatly with secateurs or scissors and not broken off.

5.7 " Sugar " should not be applied so that it renders tree-trunks and other vegetation unnecessarily unsightly.

5.8 Exercise particular care when working for rare species, e.g. by searching for larvae rather than beating for them.

5.9 Remember the Country Code!

6. Breeding

6.1 Breeding from a fertilized female or pairing in captivity is preferable to taking a series of specimens in the field.

6.2 Never collect more larvae or other livestock than can be supported by the available supply of foodplant.

6.3 Unwanted insects that have been reared should be released in the original locality, not just anywhere.

6.4 Before attempting to establish new populations or " reinforce " existing ones please consult this Committee.

ATTRACTING BUTTERFLIES
TO THE GARDEN

Happily, the urge to go out into the country-side and collect butterflies to kill and mount in cabinets is in decline and naturalists now have a more responsible attitude to the conservation not only of butterflies but of all kinds of living things. The ever-increasing pressures on wildlife have made this change of attitude both timely and essential.

Butterflies have suffered most from the destruction of suitable habitats. As towns spread outwards year by year, more and more countryside is taken for building houses and factories. Where it is not used for these purposes it is farmed more intensively than before, so that hedgerows, copses and other wild areas, which were formerly places where butterflies and their caterpillars could feed, have disappeared.

Those who enjoy the beauty of living butter-flies can continue to do so, and at the same time help to conserve them, by making their own gardens into butterfly sanctuaries. This can be done in two ways: by having plants that attract adult butterflies, and by providing food-plants for the caterpillars.

Butterfly Plants

Most butterflies in their adult stage feed only on nectar and are attracted to flowers that provide this sweet liquid in an easily accessible way. One has only to watch the activities of butterfly visitors to an ordinary garden in spring, summer or autumn to realize that a great many kinds of plants are visited by butterflies. If they are watched closely the insects will be seen to uncoil their long proboscis or tongue and insert it into the depths of the flower, remaining in this position for perhaps several minutes, and then fly on to another flower to repeat the process. The nectar which they are drinking at these times is produced by glands called nectaries which are situated in different parts of flowers depending on the species. In some they are on the calyx of the flower, in others on the petals, while in still others, such as the wallflowers, they occur at the bases of the stamens.

It should, perhaps, be mentioned that not all butterflies feed on nectar. Some sip the sap of trees, others, such as some of the Hairstreaks, drink honey-dew, the sweet excretion of aphids, and one or two, notably the splendid Purple Emperor, suck the juices from the rotting corpses of dead animals.

However, most of the butterflies which are such attractive visitors to gardens are feeders on nectar and come readily to the plants which secrete it, attracted it is believed mainly by sight and scent, and this should be borne in mind when choosing plants to include in the butterfly garden. White flowers do not seem so attractive to butterflies as pink, yellow or purplish flowers and it would make an interesting experiment to count in a garden the number of visits paid to flowers of different colours.

What, then, are the best plants to grow in a small garden to attract butterflies? Of the flowering shrubs, probably the best known for this purpose is the Butterfly Bush, *Buddleia davidii* from China. Its long plume-shaped clusters of lilac-purple flowers may be covered with butterflies in late summer. It grows readily in all places and there are a number of attractive colour varieties with rich-reddish purple flowers, blue flowers with an orange eye and pure white flowers.

A related species, *Buddleia globosa*, from Peru and Chile, has the advantage of flowering earlier in the year, in May and June. It is also semi-evergreen and produces perfumed orange-yellow flowers in globular heads. *Buddleia alternifolia* from China has long arching branches bearing sweet-scented lavender-blue flowers in small rounded clusters which are carried on the previous year's growth. These appear in June.

The many species of lilac are much visited by butterflies and most thrive in small town gardens. The Common Lilac, *Syringa vulgaris*, from Eastern Europe, bears fragrant lilac flowers in pyramidal clusters during May and June. There are many varieties with colours ranging from blue to red, and, of course, white.

The male catkins of Sallow, or "Pussy-willow", produce nectar early in spring and are useful for providing food for butterflies emerging from hibernation.

Lavender is an attractive plant, alike to gardeners and to butterflies. It has the advantage of taking up much less space in a small garden than the other flowering shrubs that have been mentioned. As an edging to a path it is a great attraction to any garden from July to September. Old English Lavender, *Lavandula spica* has a height and spread of 100–120 cm (39–48 in); for smaller gardens the variety *atropurpurea* is a smaller and more compact plant only about half the height and spread.

Heaths, *Erica* spp., are other plants that can be accommodated in quite a small garden and can give colour at most times of the year. They are rich in nectar and thus attractive to butterflies.

The choice of garden flowers, annual, biennial and perennial, for the butterfly garden is almost endless and the following are offered as common plants attractive to both gardeners and butterflies:

Alyssum, yellow	*Alyssum saxatile*
Aubrieta	*Aubrieta deltoidea*
Catmint	*Nepeta × faassenii*
Honesty	*Lunaria annua*
Michaelmas Daisy	*Aster* species
Mignonette	*Reseda odorata*
Polyanthus	*Primula × variabilis*
Primrose	*Primula vulgaris*
Sweet Rocket	*Hesperis matronalis*
Sweet William	*Dianthus barbatus*
Thrift, or	
Sea Pink	*Armeria maritima*
Valerian, red	*Kentranthus ruber*
Wallflowers	*Cheiranthus cheiri* and
	C. allionii

A bed of ivy in a garden will provide a roost and hibernating place for butterflies.

If a gardener can bring himself or herself to leave a sizeable patch of ground to grow wild this will be attractive to butterflies. Clovers, dandelions, knapweeds, ragwort and thistles are among many common weeds visited by them.

FOOD-PLANTS FOR CATERPILLARS

Having once provided plants to attract adult butterflies to a garden, the next stage is to provide food-plants for the larvae of those species that have been attracted. Butterflies, except the few species that migrate, such as the Red Admiral and Painted Lady, in general do not wander far from a chosen habitat so that once a garden has proved attractive to them and has food for both adults and larvae, they will probably remain there for many generations.

Except for the cabbage family, which attracts perhaps the only butterflies to the garden which are not welcome—the Large White and Small White—the food plants for caterpillars are mainly wild plants, and a wild patch of ground is almost essential if butterflies are to lay their eggs and remain as caterpillars in the garden.

Almost every garden will have its patch of nettles—perhaps on the site of an old manure-heap or behind a garden shed. If this can be allowed to remain during the annual garden tidying-up it will provide a splendid nursery for some of our loveliest butterflies: the Red Admiral, Painted Lady, Small Tortoiseshell, Peacock and occasionally Comma. The nettles become coarse and unattractive in high summer and so it is a good plan to cut down part of a nettle-bed about June to provide fresh young shoots for later broods of caterpillars.

Grasses of several kinds are the food-plants of the caterpillars of a number of common species including the Wall, Grayling, Meadow Brown and Small Heath butterflies. A rough patch of grass left uncut will encourage some of these species.

The list that follows includes a selection of common and easily recognized wild plants, some of which will grow naturally in gardens and will readily do so if seed is collected in the country-side and either sown directly into the ground or preferably in pots or seed-boxes and planted out later. Perhaps it should be pointed out that it is now illegal to dig up any wild plant without the permission of the owner or occupier of the land on which it is growing, but this should be readily given for common species where they are growing abundantly.

FOOD-PLANTS OF CATERPILLARS

Common name	Scientific name	Caterpillar(s)
Wallflower	*Cheiranthus cheiri*	Green-veined White
Cuckoo-flower or Lady's Smock	*Cardamine pratensis*	Green-veined White; Orange-tip
Winter Cress	*Barbarea vulgaris*	Green-veined White
Watercress	*Nasturtium officinale*	Small White, Green-veined White, Orange-tip
Hedge Garlic or Jack-by-the-Hedge	*Alliaria petiolata*	Small White, Green-veined White, Orange-tip
Charlock	*Sinapis arvensis*	Small White, Orange-tip
Sweet Rocket or Dame's Violet	*Hesperis matronalis*	Orange-tip
Horseradish	*Armoracia rusticana*	Small White, Green-veined White, Orange-tip
Wild Mignonette	*Reseda lutea*	Small White, Green-veined White
Sea Rocket	*Cakile maritima*	Green-veined White
Gorse	*Ulex europaeus* and *U. minor*	Green Hairstreak
Dyer's Greenweed	*Genista tinctoria*	Green Hairstreak
Broom	*Sarothamnus scoparius*	Green Hairstreak
Restharrow	*Ononis repens*	Common Blue
Red Clover	*Trifolium pratense*	Common Blue
White Clover	*Trifolium repens*	Common Blue
Bird's-foot Trefoil	*Lotus corniculatus*	Common Blue
Kidney Vetch	*Anthyllis vulneraria*	Small Blue
Bird's-foot Vetch	*Ornithopus perpusillus*	Common Blue

42

Bramble	*Rubus fruticosus*	Holly Blue, Green Hairstreak
Burnet-saxifrage	*Pimpinella saxifraga*	Common Blue
Ivy	*Hedera helix*	Holly Blue
Common Cudweed	*Filago vulgaris*	Painted Lady
Yarrow	*Achillea millefolium*	Common Blue
Common Ragwort	*Senecio jacobaea*	Small Copper
Burdock	*Arctium lappa*	Painted Lady
Thistles	*Cirsium* spp.	Painted Lady
Bilberry or		
Whortleberry	*Vaccinium myrtillus*	Green Hairstreak
Viper's Bugloss	*Echium vulgare*	Painted Lady
Docks	*Rumex* spp.	Small Copper
Sorrels	*Rumex* spp.	Small Copper
Nettle	*Urtica dioica*	Red Admiral, Painted Lady, Small Tortoiseshell, Peacock, Comma,
Pellitory	*Parietaria judaica*	Red Admiral
Wild Hop	*Humulus lupulus*	Red Admiral, Peacock, Comma
Smooth Meadow Grass	*Poa pratensis*	Meadow Brown
Holly	*Ilex aquifolium*	Holly Blue
Spindle	*Euonymus europaeus*	Holly Blue
Buckthorn	*Rhamnus catharticus*	Green Hairstreak, Brimstone
Alder Buckthorn	*Frangula alnus*	Holly Blue, Green Hairstreak, Brimstone
Dogwood	*Swida sanguinea*	Holly Blue, Green Hairstreak

Fig. 10

Larvae-collecting tins and glass-topped tins for eggs
and young caterpillars.

Introducing Butterflies to the Garden

The establishment of a butterfly garden can
be speeded up by introducing common and
suitable species from the surrounding country-
side. It is not usually satisfactory to release adult
butterflies themselves as they will rarely settle
down in unfamiliar surroundings, but a captive
female can sometimes be induced to lay its eggs
if the correct food-plant is placed in a large box
or small tub, and the insect released in it. The
top of the box must, of course, be covered with
fine netting. The resulting caterpillars can be
reared either by " sleeving " or in rearing cages.
A sleeve is a large tube of muslin open at both

44

FIG. 11

Breeding Cage.

ends which is slipped over the growing plant. After introducing the caterpillars the tube is tied at both ends. It must be moved to a fresh spray of leaves from time to time.

Very young caterpillars can be reared more satisfactorily at first in small glass-topped tins as shown in Fig. 10. A popular type of breeding cage for later use is illustrated in Fig. 11. These, and other equipment for butterfly rearing, are available from dealers in natural history supplies.

Caterpillars in the wild suffer severely from parasites—insects of two orders: Hymenoptera (ichneumons, chalcids and braconids) and Diptera (tachinids). The parasites lay their eggs either on the skin of the caterpillars or inside their bodies. The parasitic larvae eat the tissues of the hosts and eventually kill them. If butterfly eggs or very young caterpillars can be found before they have been attacked by parasites, you are likely to rear more butterflies than would survive in natural conditions; if so, some can be released back into the wild.

The Small Tortoiseshell is a good butterfly to start rearing. Its food-plant – nettles – is only too easily obtainable, and you may be lucky enough to find in June a batch of eggs or a web with a mass of young caterpillars, recently hatched, on the nettles in your garden, or in the countryside. There will also be a second brood in August, but some of these will hibernate and only emerge in spring.

When rearing caterpillars in the small boxes, fresh leaves of the food-plant must be provided every day; the young insects will leave the stale leaves for the new ones. The old leaves and frass (excrement) must be removed daily.

In rearing cages the food-plant can be either a growing specimen in a pot, if it is a small plant, or a bunch of leaves and stems standing in water, in a wide-based but narrow-necked jar. To prevent the caterpillars getting drowned if they fall off the plant, a tuft of cotton-wool can be pushed into the neck of the jar each time a fresh supply of leaves is put in.

The top of the plant should be clear of the roof of the breeding cage. When caterpillars of species such as the Small Tortoiseshell and Red Admiral change to pupae they will want to hang down from the top of the cage. Do not leave breeding cages in direct sunlight, or the food-plant may wilt and possibly cause digestive troubles in the caterpillars.

Readers who are unable to find their own insects can order eggs or pupae from a number of butterfly farms. The butterfly farms supply the eggs or pupae at the appropriate time of year, with full instructions for rearing.

Fuller information on rearing butterflies and other insects for releasing in gardens will be found in *Studying Insects*, by R. L. E. Ford (Warne, 1973).

REVISED LIST OF BUTTERFLIES

For the 1977 and subsequent impressions of this book the scientific names of the British butterflies have been altered to conform to the new edition of Kloet (G.S.) and Hinks (W.D.) *A Check List of British Insects* (1972), but the families throughout the text are arranged in reverse order of this list, beginning with the most specialized species and ending with the most primitive.

pre 1934	*post 1972*
HESPERIIDAE	
Carterocephalus palaemon	No alteration
Adopoea thaumas .	. *Thymelicus sylvestris*
Adopoea lineola .	. *Thymelicus lineola*
Adopoea arteon .	. *Thymelicus acteon*
Augiades comma .	. *Hesperia comma*
Augiades sylvanus .	. *Ochlodes venata*
Thanaos tages .	. *Erynnis tages*
Hesperia malvae .	. *Pyrgus malvae*
PAPILIONIDAE	
Papilio machaon .	. No alteration
PIERIDAE	
Leptosia sinapis .	. *Leptidea sinapis*
Colias hyale .	. No alteration
Colias australis .	. ,,
Colias edusa .	. *Colias croceus*

48

pre 1934	*post 1972*

PIERIDAE—*continued.*

Gonepteryx rhamni .	No alteration
Aporia crataegi . .	,,
Pieris brassicae . .	,,
Pieris rapae . .	,,
Pieris napi . . .	,,
Pontia daplidice . .	,,
Euchloë cardamines .	*Anthocharis cardamines*

LYCAENIDAE

Callophrys rubi . .	No alteration
Zephyrus betulae .	*Thecla betulae*
Thecla quercus .	*Quercusia quercus*
Strymon w-album .	*Strymonidia w-album*
Strymon pruni .	*Strymonidia pruni*
Chrysophanus dispar .	*Lycaena dispar*
Chrysophanus phlaeas .	*Lycaena phlaeas*
Cosmolyce boeticus .	*Lampides boeticus*
Zizera minima .	*Cupido minimus*
Cupido argiades .	*Everes argiades*
Lycaena argus .	*Plebejus argus*
Lycaena astrarche .	*Aricia agestis*
Lycaena icarus .	*Polyommatus icarus*
Lycaena corydon .	*Lysandra coridon*
Lycaena bellargus .	*Lysandra bellargus*
Nomiades semiargus .	*Cyaniris semiargus*
Nomiades arion .	*Maculinea arion*
Cyaniris argiolus . .	*Celastrina argiolus*

pre 1934   *post 1972*

RIODINIDAE (= ERYCINIDAE)   NEMEOBIIDAE

Nemeobius lucina .   .   *Hamearis lucina*

NYMPHALIDAE

Limenitis sibylla .	*Ladoga camilla*
Apatura iris	No alteration
Pyrameis atalanta	*Vanessa atalanta*
Pyrameis cardui .	*Vanessa cardui*
Vanessa urticae .	*Aglais urticae*
Vanessa polychloros	*Nymphalis polychloros*
Vanessa antiopa .	*Nymphalis antiopa*
Vanessa io .	*Inachis io*
Polygonia c-album	No alteration
Argynnis selene .	*Boloria (Clossiana) selene*
Argynnis euphrosyne	*Boloria (Clossiana) euphrosyne*
Argynnis lathonia	*Argynnis (Issoria) lathonia*
Argynnis cydippe .	*Argynnis (Fabriciana) adippe*
Argynnis aglaia .	*Argynnis (Mesoacidalia) aglaja*
Argynnis paphia .	*Argynnis (Argynnis) paphia*
Melitaea aurinia .	*Euphydryas aurinia*
Melitaea cinxia .	No alteration
Melitaea athalia .	*Mellicta athalia*

pre 1934   *post 1972*

SATYRIDAE

pre 1934	post 1972
Pararge egeria	*Pararge aegeria*
Pararge megaera	*Lasiommata megera*
Erebia epiphron	No alteration
Erebia aethiops	,,
Agapetes galathea	*Melanargia galathea*
Satyrus semele	*Hipparchia semele*
Epinephele tithonus	*Pyronia tithonus*
Epinephele ianira	*Maniola jurtina*
Coenonympha pamphilus	No alteration
Coenonympha typhon	*Coenonympha tullia*
Aphantopus hyperantus	No alteration

DANAIDAE

Anosia plexippus	*Danaus plexippus*

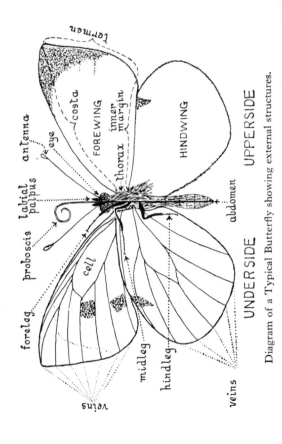

Diagram of a Typical Butterfly showing external structures.

UPPERSIDE

UNDERSIDE

termen

costa

inner margin

FOREWING

HINDWING

thorax

abdomen

antenna

eye

labial palpus

proboscis

foreleg

cell

veins

midleg

hindleg

veins

THE MILKWEED BUTTERFLY

Family DANAIDAE   *Danaus plexippus*

This species is undoubtedly migratory in its habits and was first observed in England in 1876 since when its appearance has been very irregular, but in 1968 sixty-two were reported from the southern counties.

The pale green egg is conical in shape with upright ridges and many cross lines and is laid singly on various kinds of milkweed, usually upon the under-surface of the leaves.

The caterpillar has a yellow head banded with black. The naked body is white with numerous black and yellow transverse stripes and with a pair of long black filaments on the 2nd segment and a shorter pair on the 8th.

The chrysalis is smooth and rounded without striking prominences.

The butterfly is brownish orange with black veins and black margins on all the wings, a double row of white spots on the outer margins and seven larger ones on the black apical patch of the forewings. The male (illustrated) has a small patch of black androconial scales on the second median nervure of each hind wing.

THE MILKWEED BUTTERFLY

THE SPECKLED WOOD BUTTERFLY

Family SATYRIDAE   *Pararge aegeria*

This species is generally distributed throughout England and Wales, more plentiful in the south and west than in the east and north ; everywhere abundant in Ireland, local in Scotland and rare north of the Caledonian Canal.

It is usually found to frequent shady lanes, borders of woods, etc., where the sun's rays are more or less intercepted by a leafy screen, and seems to be more abundant in wet seasons than in dry ones.

The butterfly is blackish-brown in colour and the spots are yellowish. There is one white-pupilled black eye spot near the tips of the fore wings and three such spots on the outer area of the hind wings. The female (illustrated) is usually slightly larger than the male and the yellowish spots distinctly larger. The spots are sometimes much reduced in size in the male, or greatly enlarged in the female.

The egg is pale greenish and finely reticulated. As the caterpillar matures within, the shell becomes less glossy than at first, and the upper part is blackish.

THE SPECKLED WOOD BUTTERFLY

The caterpillar has a green head which is larger than the first ring of the body and is covered with short whitish hairs with which are mixed a few dark hairs. The body is rather a brighter green, with darker lines, edged with yellowish, along the

back and sides. The skin is wrinkled and the whole of the body is clothed with whitish hair and a few dark hairs arising from warts ; the anal points are also hairy. It feeds on various grasses, among which are Couch and Cock's-foot.

The chrysalis is pale green, tinged with yellowish or whitish ; the edges of the wing covers are brown and there are whitish dots on the body. These colours may vary. It is suspended by the cremaster from a silken pad.

From eggs laid in early May butterflies appeared at the end of June ; and from eggs laid in June butterflies resulted in the middle of August. Early July eggs produced perfect insects in early September, and from caterpillars fed up in October butterflies were out in November.

THE WALL BUTTERFLY

Family SATYRIDAE   *Lasiommata megera*

A sunshine loving species fond of basking on walls, dry hedge-banks, sides of gravel-pits, tree trunks, etc.; in fact, wherever it can enjoy the full sunshine. It may be regarded as a generally common species in the southern, eastern, and

western counties; more local in the north, and in south-west Scotland it seems fairly distributed.

The egg is pale green when first laid and almost spherical in shape. It is finely ribbed and reticulated.

The caterpillar when full grown is whitish-green dotted with white. From the larger of these dots on the back arise greyish bristles; the three lines on the back are whitish, edged with dark green; the line on the sides is white, fringed with greyish hairs; anal points green, hairy, and extreme tips white. Head, larger than the first segment, is green, hairy, and dotted with white. It feeds on various grasses such as Couch and Cock's-foot.

The chrysalis is green, with yellow-tinted white markings on the edge of the wing covers and ridges; the spots on the body are yellowish. Occasionally the chrysalids are blackish with white or yellow points on the body. It hangs suspended from a grass stem.

THE WALL BUTTERFLY

The butterfly is bright fulvous in colour, with blackish-brown veins, margins and transverse lines. There is one white-pupilled black spot on the fore wings, and four similar spots on the outer area of the hind wings. The male has a very conspicuous sexual brand on the central area The female (left wing) has more ample wings and as the sexual brand is absent in this sex the central black transverse lines are more distinct.

Variation is chiefly in the size and number of the spots. The central transverse lines on the fore wings of the female are sometimes broad and occasionally the space between the lines is blackish. The ground colour also varies in tint, darker or lighter than normal and specimens of very light shades are known to occur.

There are certainly two broods of this butterfly in the season, and in favourable years there may be three. In an ordinary way they will be on the wing in May and June and the second flight in July and August.

THE SMALL MOUNTAIN RINGLET
BUTTERFLY

Family SATYRIDAE   *Erebia epiphron*

As is indicated by its English name, this interesting little butterfly frequents only high ground and is rarely found below about 1,500 feet. All its English localities are in the Lake District of Cumbria. It seems to prefer boggy ground. In such places on Gable Hill, Red Screes, and at Langdale Pikes, among others, it is not uncommon. It is also known to occur, sometimes in abundance, on Ben Nevis and other adjacent hills; also in suitable spots at the proper elevation around Lochs Rannoch and Vennachar, as well as in the Tay district and Argyllshire. It has been recorded from Ireland but has probably died out there.

The butterfly is deep velvety brown and has the tawny bands on the fore wings broken up by the nervures into oval blotches with central black dots and a lesser number of similar blotches on the hind wings. The female generally is somewhat larger than the male, with the bands or rings paler. Variation in the markings is extensive. The usual form found in the British Isles is subspecies *aetherius*, while true *epiphron*, if it exists, is exceedingly rare.

The egg, when first laid, is yellow, changing

afterwards to fawn colour with darker markings, especially towards the top. It is laid in July on blades of grass. The larva hatches in about sixteen days.

The young caterpillar, before hibernation in October, is greenish, with darker green and

yellow lines. The head is brownish in tint. It feeds both before and after hibernation on various grasses, with a distinct preference for Mat Grass which appears to be the natural food.

The chrysalis is a little more than three-eights of an inch in length, rather thick in proportion. The colour of the back of the thorax and wing cases is a light green, rather glaucous ; the abdomen a pale drab or dirty whitish ; a dark brown dorsal streak is conspicuous on the thorax and there is a faint indication of a dark brown stripe along the abdomen. The pupa is placed low down among grass stems which are loosely spun together.

THE SCOTCH ARGUS BUTTERFLY

Family SATYRIDAE   *Erebia aethiops*

This butterfly occurs only in Scotland and not now in England. Its haunt is the margin of a plantation or wood where the different species of *Poa* grass grow abundantly, and always situated where it receives the first rays of the rising sun.

The insect is truly sun loving, and it is almost useless to search for it if the day be dull. It is extremely sensible to shine and shade. A good day to illustrate this is one when clouds at intervals obscure the sun ; the moment it disappears so also does the butterfly, and no sooner does it shine forth again than, as if by magic, scores of the insect are on the wing.

The egg is roundish and ochreous-white in colour, finely freckled with pale brown or pinkish-brown ; it has a number of ribs and is also reticulated.

The caterpillar in its last skin is pale drab, the warts pale whitish-brown with short bristles ; dorsal stripe blackish-brown enclosed by two paler lines ; subdorsal stripe paler drab, becoming narrow towards the anal point, edged above with a greenish-brown thread, and below with blackish or brownish dashes ; below this come two thin pale lines, above the lower of which are the circular black spiracles. The under parts are of

THE SCOTCH ARGUS BUTTERFLY

a warmer tint of the ground colour of the back. It is a nocturnal feeder, coming up to feed on various grasses at dusk.

The chrysalis has the body ochreous, with a darker stripe down the back. It is placed in a loose open network cocoon in a more or less upright position.

The typical male butterfly (illustrated) is deep velvety brown, appearing almost black in very fresh specimens. There is a broad fulvous band on the outer area of the fore wings, the upper part has two white-pupilled black spots, and the lower part has one such spot. The hind wings have a narrow fulvous band, usually enclosing three white-pupilled black spots. The female is generally less dark and velvety, the bands are rather wider, more orange in colour, and the white pupils of the spots are more conspicuous. There are, however, many modifications of the markings of this local species showing its very variable character.

THE MARBLED WHITE BUTTERFLY

Family SATYRIDAE   *Melanargia galathea*

This species is found in most of the midland counties and in nearly all of the southern ones, but is especially common on the chalk downs of the south-west. It does not occur in Scotland or Ireland, and seems to be absent from the northern counties of England except Yorkshire. It is reported to be not uncommon in three localities not far from York. The butterflies usually affect broken ground, rough fields, grassy slopes near woods, or even sunny banks on the edges of corn-fields. They keep pretty much together so that a selection of a series on the spot is quite an easy matter and can be effected without destroying a single specimen over and above the required number.

The ground colour of the butterfly is creamy-white and the markings are blackish ; the eye spots which are not always in evidence on the upper side are well defined on the under side, especially so on the hind wings.

The female is generally whiter and larger than

the male and has the basal half of the front margin of the fore wings ochreous brown. Variation consists chiefly of increase or decrease in the size of the blackish markings and the ground colour is sometimes decidedly yellow.

The egg is whitish and opaque, with a dark speck on the apex ; the base is flattened and slightly hollowed, and it is finely reticulated, but without distinct striations or anything resembling ribs. The eggs are laid in July and are not attached to anything.

The caterpillar when full grown is whity-brown in colour with brownish lines. The head is brown tinged with pink and the tail-like points on the last ring are pink. The head, as well as the body, is clothed with short hair.

Sheep's-fescue, Cock's-foot, and Cat's-tail grasses are given as food plants, but caterpillars in confinement seem to eat any kind of grass that is supplied. When full-fed in June it changes to a pupa without suspending itself in any way, or making a cocoon.

The chrysalis is also whity-brown with a pinkish tinge and browner speckling on the wing cases, and the body is marked down the back with yellow. It is placed loose amongst the grass-roots.

THE GRAYLING BUTTERFLY

Family SATYRIDAE   *Hipparchia semele*

This species occurs in almost every county in England and Wales, as far north as Sutherland-shire in Scotland, and is widely distributed in Ireland. It delights in sitting rather than flying about cliffs and sand-hills, heaths and downs, and

even open woodlands. It is fond of sunning itself on rocks. The under sides of the hind wings agree so admirably in colour and marking with the soil, etc., that although one may watch it settle a few yards away, it is not to be seen when one reaches the spot. When disturbed it starts up, flies a short distance, and then repeats the dis-appearing trick. It is said to have a fancy for the resinous sap that oozes from pine trees. Flowers of thyme, heather, etc., are also attractive.

The egg is of a dull creamy tint, strongly ribbed and with a slight depression on the top. The eggs are laid early in August on the blades and stems of grasses.

The caterpillar when full grown is drab in tint, delicately mottled, with brownish longitudinal stripes broadest along the middle segments. The spiracular stripe is broad and the spiracles are black. The head is brown. It feeds on various grasses.

The chrysalis is rounded and smooth and wholly of a deep red mahogany colour, and placed in a

THE GRAYLING BUTTERFLY

hollow space just below the surface of the ground and close to the roots of grass.

The butterfly is brown, more or less suffused with black, especially on the outer area of the wings of the male. The fore wings have two white-pupilled spots and there is one black spot towards the anal angle which may be pupilled with white. The female (left wing), apart from its larger size and brighter bands, may be distinguished from the male by the absence of the blackish brand on the disc of the fore wings. Variation is largely confined to the under side of the hind wings, which are so coloured and marked as to provide a perfect camouflage for the insect's protection from its enemies when resting.

THE GATEKEEPER BUTTERFLY

Family SATYRIDAE   *Pyronia tithonus*

The Gatekeeper is generally distributed throughout England and is often very plentiful in the southern counties and also in South Wales. It is doubtful if it occurs in Scotland. In Ireland it is confined to the southern area.

The general colour of the butterfly is brownish-orange and the margins of the wings are fuscous-brown. There is a black spot towards the tips of the fore wings, as a rule enclosing two white dots, one or both of these dots sometimes absent in the male. The female (left wing) differs from the male in its rather larger size. There is usually a white-pupilled black spot towards the anal angle of the hind wing of both sexes, but sometimes this spot is absent. Colour changes occur, and the orange colour, in both sexes, may be replaced by yellow or even white. But such aberrations are very local and rare. They are on the wing in July and August, and may be seen, sometimes in considerable numbers, where the rides are grassy, in woods, but they are, perhaps, more attached to

67

hedgerows. Bramble flowers are their special attraction, but they are not indifferent to the blossoms of the Wood Sage or of Marjoram.

The egg, when first laid is pale yellowish,  becoming lighter in tint and irregularly blotched with reddish-brown, the upper blotches forming a sort of band round the egg ; as the caterpillar matures the shell assumes a darker tinge, and the markings are less distinct.

The caterpillar, when full grown, is pale ochreous, clothed with short pale hair, and freckled with brownish ; the line down the back is darker, one on each side is paler, and that above the feet is yellowish. The head is bristly and rather darker than the body. The caterpillar feeds at night on various grasses, such as Cock's-foot and Couch.

The chrysalis is whitish-ochreous, with dark brown streaks on the wing covers and some brownish spots and clouds on the back and sides. It is suspended from a stem or blade of grass and the old skin remains attached.

THE MEADOW BROWN BUTTERFLY

Family SATYRIDAE   *Maniola jurtina*

From its wide distribution and general abundance the Meadow Brown may be said to be our commonest butterfly, and is found throughout England and Wales, Scotland, including the Isles of Lewis and Orkney, also Ireland. It appears to be always on the wing, in dull weather as well as sunshine, and except for a short interval in early August, is to be seen in hayfields, open spaces in woods, or borders of highways and byways from June to September.

The egg, whitish-green in colour at first, inclines to brownish-yellow as it matures and is marked with purplish-brown. It is upright and ribbed with the top flattened and an impressed ring. It is laid on a blade of grass.

The caterpillar is bright green, clothed with short whitish hairs ; there is a darker line down the back and a diffused white stripe on each side above the reddish spiracles ; the anal points are white. The head is rather darker green and hairy. It feeds on various kinds of grasses at night in May.

The chrysalis is pale green, marked with brownish on the wing covers, the thorax is spotted with blackish, and the points on the body are brownish. It is suspended and with the old skin attached.

THE MEADOW BROWN BUTTERFLY

This fuscous-brown butterfly is marked with dull orange, especially in the female. The male (right wing) has a broad black sexual brand on the central area of the fore wings, and a white-pupilled black spot towards the tips of the wings ; this spot is usually encircled with orange and there is often more or less of this orange colour below it. The female is without the black brand and is more ornamented with orange, which generally forms a broad patch on the outer area of the fore wings, but it is sometimes continued inwards so that almost the whole of the fore wings, except the margins, appear to be orange. Sometimes, generally in the male, the apical spot is entirely absent, or is greatly reduced in size, and is without the white pupil.

Altogether this species is subject to rather extensive variation.

THE SMALL HEATH BUTTERFLY

Family SATYRIDAE   *Coenonympha pamphilus*

This interesting little butterfly is to be seen almost everywhere, but it is, perhaps, most frequently to be found on grassy places in lanes, heaths and downs, rough meadows, etc.   It occurs on mountains even up to an elevation of 600 m (2,000 ft).   It rests and sleeps on grass or rushes.

A common species throughout England, Wales, Scotland, as far north as Nairn, and the Outer Hebrides, also Ireland.

The wings of the butterfly are pale tawny, with a brownish border, of variable width, on all the wings, and stronger in the male than the female ; there is a black spot towards the tip of each fore wing.   Variation in this species is extensive but not striking.   The tint of the ground colour may be reddish or yellowish ; occasionally brownish specimens of the male occur.   The female (illustrated) is in all cases paler, and somewhat larger than the male, and is sometimes whitish-ochreous in colour.   The brown border is also a variable character and may be very dark and broad or reduced to linear proportions.   The apical spot may be of fair size and very black or very pale and indistinct or entirely absent.

THE SMALL HEATH BUTTERFLY

The egg is green at first, afterwards becoming whitish ; later on a brownish ring appears a little above the middle, and there are brownish freckles. It is finely ribbed and the top is depressed, forming

a hollow. They are sometimes laid in a cluster of four on a blade of grass, others are deposited singly, all in mid-June.

The caterpillar is a clear green colour with a darker green dorsal stripe, with the spiracular stripe not so dark ; the anal points are pink.

The chrysalis is a delicate pale yellowish-green with a faintly darker green dorsal stripe ; wing covers edged with whitish, outlined with reddish-brown ; abdomen freckled with paler green ; wing-cases faintly marked with darker green. It is suspended from a grass blade or stalk.

Some caterpillars, from eggs laid in May or June, become full-grown in four or five weeks, and appear as butterflies in August, but others do not complete their growth until the following spring.

THE LARGE HEATH BUTTERFLY

Family SATYRIDAE   *Coenonympha tullia*

The present distribution of this species is much reduced but it occurs in the " mosses " of Lancashire and Cheshire and the moors of Yorkshire. Northward it is found in all suitable

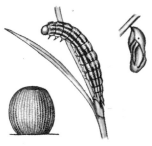

mosses and moors in Durham and Cumbria. In Scotland and Ireland it is generally distributed and occurs up to an elevation of 600 m (2,000 ft). In some localities in North Wales it is not uncommon.

The egg is very pale greenish-yellow at first, but the green fades, brownish blotches appear, and some dark markings appear a short while before the caterpillar hatches out. It is finely scored and the top is depressed with a raised boss in the centre.

The full grown caterpillar is described as bright green with a dark bluish-green dorsal line, edged with pale yellow,, the spiracular lines are also pale yellow and the caudal fork is tipped with pink.

The chrysalis is bright green, with brown streaks on the edges and centre of the wing covers and at the tail, turning brown just before the butterfly emerges.

The butterfly is a most variable one, both as regards colour and marking, and many inter-

mediate forms and varieties exist. In the typical form the colour ranges from darkish-brown to pale tawny ; there is an ochreous ringed black spot towards the tips of the fore wings, sometimes another similar spot above the inner angle, and occasionally when both spots are present there is an ochreous spot between them. The hind wings have from one to three or more of similar spots. The female is much paler and slightly larger than the male (illustrated).

The eggs are laid in July on blades of grass and the caterpillars hatch out in that month and August. The food of the caterpillar is said to be the Beak Sedge, but it feeds also on various kinds of meadow grass. After hibernation they recommence feeding and are full-grown in May and June, when they pupate, and the butterflies appear at the end of June and in July.

THE RINGLET BUTTERFLY

Family SATYRIDAE   *Aphantopus hyperantus*

This species may be found throughout the greater part of England and Wales. It is fairly plentiful in most of the southern counties of Scotland, and its range extends north to Aberdeen. In Ireland it is abundant in the south and west. It frequents shady lanes and the outskirts of woods and usually flies along the shady side, but it is not averse to the nectar of the Bramble blossom, fully exposing itself to sunshine all the time.

The butterfly is rather sombre-looking ; all the wings are sooty-brown, the male when quite fresh appearing almost black and the sexual brand then difficult to see ; there are one or more black spots with pale rings, and sometimes white pupils, on the fore wings, but these are always more prominent in the female (illustrated) ; they may be entirely absent in the male. On the under side there are generally two, sometimes three, spots on the fore wings and five spots on the hind wings. There is much variation in the matter of size of these spots. The butterflies are on the wing in July and August.

THE RINGLET BUTTERFLY

The egg is yellowish-white at first, but soon turns to a pale brown. They are not attached to anything, but are allowed to fall down among the  roots of the grass over which they are deposited.

The caterpillar is pale brown in colour with a darker line down the back and a whitish stripe above the feet, and the head has three broad dark stripes on each cheek. It feeds upon various grasses, such as Cock's-foot and Couch growing about damp places in woodland districts. It emerges from the egg in August, feeds leisurely until October, when partial hibernation occurs. If the weather is suitable the larva will take small feeds during this period. In March it resumes feeding but does not attain full growth until June.

The chrysalis is ochreous-brown sprinkled with reddish-brown, and marked with brown on the wing covers. It lies low down among the grass roots in a very slight cocoon.

THE SMALL PEARL-BORDERED FRITILLARY

Family NYMPHALIDAE   *Boloria (Clossiana) selene*

Throughout England and Wales this species is fairly common but rather local, and is often abundant in some of the more extensive woods of the southern counties, but it also seems to have a fondness for the margins of brooks, where these run through or by the sides of woods. It occurs in Scotland and is not uncommon in Sutherlandshire.

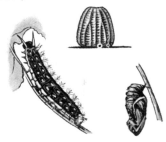

One specimen only recorded from Ireland.

The egg is at first greenish, then yellowish, and afterwards greyish, and then becoming blackish towards the hollowed top. It bears ribs, eighteen or twenty in number and is laid in June or July on plants of the Dog Violet.

The young caterpillar, on emerging from the egg, devours most of the shell. It is then a pale olive colour with brownish warts, from each of which there is a rather long jointed bristle ; the head is black. When full-grown it is a smoky-pink colour and velvety-looking. There is a brownish line along the middle of the back. The spines are ochreous in colour and beset with fine pointed black bristles, the two spines on the first ring are rather more than twice the length of the others, and are directed forward. A pinkish

THE SMALL PEARL-BORDERED FRITILLARY

stripe runs along the lower part of the body, just above the feet. Head black and notched on the crown.

The chrysalis is brown on the thorax and body; the wing cases ochreous and marked with black near the edge. It is suspended from a pad of silk spun on a stem or leaf-stalk.

The butterfly is a bright, rather deep, fulvous colour with black markings. The female is rather larger and slightly more orange in tint than the male (illustrated) and has a series of pale spots on the outer margin of each wing. There is much variation in both colour and markings. Variation consists of more or less black suffusion on the basal or general area of the wings and an increase in the size of the black spots, resulting in the formation of bands or patches; or the black spots may be much reduced in size, and some of them entirely absent. The usual colour is sometimes replaced by yellowish or whitish-buff tints; occasionally white spots appear on the wings.

THE PEARL-BORDERED FRITILLARY

Family NYMPHALIDAE *Boloria (Clossiana)*
euphrosyne

The Pearl-bordered Fritillary is generally
common in woods in England and Wales, abundant in the southern counties. It used to be
plentiful in Northumberland and Durham, but
has become scarce in those counties. It is not
uncommon in some districts in Scotland and
occurs in Co. Clare, Ireland.

The colour and markings of the butterfly are
bright fulvous with black spots and veins. There
is one silvery spot at the base of the hind wings,
a larger one about the middle of the wings, and
a row of spots on the outer margin. The female
is rather larger than the male (illustrated) and
darker at the bases of the wings. There is also
much variation in the general colour and markings in this species, chiefly in the black suffusion
on the basal area of the wings and the variation
in the size of the black spots. It is usually on the
wing in May or June, but in early seasons it may
appear at the end of April.

The egg, which is laid in May or June, is
whitish-green at first, and afterwards turns
brownish. It is distinctly ribbed and the top

is somewhat rounded and hollowed in the centre.

The caterpillar, when full-grown, is black, and clothed with numerous minute hairs. There is a greyish-edged black line down the middle of the

back, and the spines on each side of this are yellowish with the tips and the branches black; all the other spines are black. A greyish stripe runs along the lower part of the sides, and this is traversed from the fourth to the last ring by a blackish line. Head black, shining, downy, and slightly notched on the crown. The natural food-plant is Dog Violet, but the caterpillar will also eat garden Pansy or leaf of Primrose. It retires for hibernation when quite small, and recommences to feed in March.

The chrysalis is brownish, with the raised parts of the head and thorax greyish; the body is paler brown, and the points are blackish. It is suspended from a pad of silk spun upon a leaf or stem.

THE QUEEN OF SPAIN FRITILLARY

Family NYMPHALIDAE   *Argynnis (Issoria)*
                                                lathonia

This migrant butterfly has been taken, chiefly
odd specimens, in many of the eastern and southern counties of England, from Norfolk to Dover
and almost always in the autumn. The neighbour-
hood of Dover seems
to have always been
the most favoured
locality. There are
two broods of the
butterfly in the year,
one in the spring
and the other in the
autumn. Females
from the Continent
may arrive on our
east or south coasts
in May and deposit eggs from which the autumn
butterflies are developed. The fate of the caterpillars from autumnal eggs would depend on the
winter ; if mild they might manage to attain the
butterfly state about May, but their doing so is
rather doubtful.

The egg, Mr. Frohawk states, is $\frac{1}{40}$th of an inch
(0·6 mm) high, of a straight-sided conical form.
There are about forty longitudinal keels of different lengths and the spaces between the keels are
ribbed transversely. A pale lemon-yellow shade
at first, inclining to ochreous, the colour gradually
deepens becoming yellower, then assumes a dull
grey, finally changing to a lilac-grey.

The full-grown caterpillar is velvety black,
densely sprinkled with white dots, each bearing a
black bristle ; there are six rows of brown spines

THE QUEEN OF SPAIN FRITILLARY

and black bristles ; two white streaks along the
back on the fore part of each ring and white warts
with black bristles on the hind part. The head
is amber-coloured above and black below and is
covered with bristles.

The chrysalis has the head, thorax, and wing
cases olive-brown ; the body speckled with brown,
ochreous, black, and white. The spiracles are
black and the points on the body amber-coloured.
It is suspended from a stem.

The butterfly, the male of which is illustrated,
in shape and in general appearance is not unlike
the Silver-washed Fritillary. The black markings
vary somewhat in size, and occasionally those on
the front area, or those on the inner area of the
fore wings, are more or less confluent ; very
rarely the wings are suffused with a steely-blue or
bronze colour.

THE DARK GREEN FRITILLARY

Family NYMPHALIDAE *Argynnis (Mesoacidalia)*
aglaja

Common locally in many of the English and
Welsh counties ; in Scotland it occurs in many
suitable districts and in Ireland it seems to be
chiefly attached to the coast. Moorlands, downs,
sea-cliffs, and flowery slopes are the kind of situations most to the fancy of this agile butterfly. It
is on the wing in July and August, and is much
more easily seen than caught. However, it is
rather fond of perching on the taller kinds of
thistles, and is then not difficult to capture, if
quietly approached.

The butterfly is bright fulvous in the male,
paler in the female generally; the latter sex is
blackish towards the base, and has paler spots on
the outer margin. There is some variation in the
tone of the ground colour, lighter or darker than
normal in both sexes ; the female seems to be the
most variable in this respect. The black spots
are apt to run together, and so form bands and
blotches.

THE DARK GREEN FRITILLARY

The egg is yellowish when first laid, and a day or two afterwards violet-brown rings appear above the base and the apical half. It is ribbed and finely cross-ribbed ; the top is slightly depressed.

The caterpillar, when full-grown, is purplish-grey, thickly mixed with velvety black ; the grey is most in evidence between the rings and along the lower part of the sides. There is a yellow stripe along the middle of the back. Along the lower part of the sides there is a row of reddish spots, connected by a yellowish line. The black spines are branched. The head is glossy black, and, like the body, hairy. It feeds on Dog Violet in May and June.

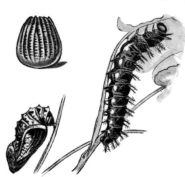

The chrysalis has the head, thorax, and wing cases black, very glossy, and marked with pale brownish ; the body is pale brownish, and the points black. It is suspended in a tent-like arrangement of leaves.

THE HIGH BROWN FRITILLARY

Family NYMPHALIDAE   *Argynnis* (*Fabriciana*)
adippe

The distribution of this species is more restricted than that of *A. aglaja*. Its extreme northern boundary is reached in Cumbria, but it has disappeared from some of its former haunts in the larger woods of southern counties from Kent, Essex, Suffolk and Norfolk to Devonshire and S. Wales ; also in the more sheltered woods of the Midlands, Yorkshire, Lancashire, and Cumbria.

The egg, when first laid, is yellowish-green ; it afterwards turns pink, and then rosy-red ; during the winter it changes to greyish- or bluish-green. As a rule, the eggs are laid at the end of July. The caterpillar is fully formed soon after the egg is laid, but remains within the shell all winter, and does not hatch until the following March or early in April.

The caterpillar feeds upon Dog Violet, and also the Sweet Violet. The head is pinkish-brown, covered with short greyish bristles. Body black, incrusted with ochreous-grey on the sides, and on the back marked with the same tint on the hinder half of each ring ; dorsal

line white. The branched spines are pinkish-brown.

The chrysalis is deep brown, freckled with paler ; points along the back of the body and the points on the thorax are brilliant greenish-golden. The wing cases are rather paler. It is suspended from a leaf or stem.

The butterfly is fulvous with black spots and veins. The female generally is not so bright in tint as the male.

The series of black spots parallel with the outer margin of the fore wing are normally six in number, but the third is usually small and sometimes absent, whilst the fourth and fifth are often much larger than the others of the series. In the corresponding row on the hind wing the first and third spots are sometimes wanting. A very rare aberration has the central area of the fore wings black. Aberrations and varieties of this species are numerous.

86

THE SILVER-WASHED FRITILLARY

Family NYMPHALIDAE   *Argynnis (Argynnis)*
paphia

This species is to be found in most of the
southern English and Welsh counties, especially
where there are extensive woods.   It is abundant
in the New Forest, and also in some parts of
Ireland.
    The wings of this fine butterfly are fulvous,
with the veins and spots black ; the spots on the
hind wings are band-like, and the central spots on
the fore wings are sometimes connected.   The
female (left wing) is paler in colour than the
male and is without the heavy black scales on
veins 1, 2, and 3 ; the basal third of the fore
wing, and a larger area of the hind wing, tinged
with greenish.   There is considerable aberration
in this species.
    The female also produces another form known
as var. *valezina*.   The fulvous ground colour in
the typical form is replaced by smoky-bronze green.

THE SILVER-WASHED FRITILLARY

The sub-apical area of the fore wings palest. *Valezina* occurs chiefly in the New Forest.

The egg, laid on tree trunks in July, is whitish tinged with green, ribbed and cross-furrowed, the alternate ribs not extending to the top. As the caterpillar matures, the egg-shell appears blackish, and the ribs hoary.

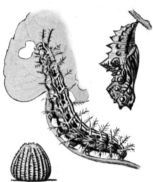

The caterpillar, when full grown, is velvety black with two bright yellow lines along the back; the spines are of a reddish-ochreous colour with the extreme tips and branches black. There are only two spines on the first ring, and these are inclined forward over the head. The caterpillar hatches in August, and after eating its egg-shell and nibbling a leaf or two of Dog Violet, goes into winter quarters whilst in its second skin; the spines have not yet appeared. In April, after feeding again, it moults the second time, and the spines are then disclosed.

The chrysalis is of a pale ochreous colour, streaked and mottled with brownish; the hollow part of the back has a brilliant golden sheen, and the points on the rest of the body are gold-tipped. It is suspended by the anal hooks to a silken pad spun on a twig or rock.

THE MARSH FRITILLARY

Family NYMPHALIDAE   *Euphydryas aurinia*

Although it has seemingly disappeared from
various English localities where it was formerly
common, this species may be found in many
parts of the British Islands, but it is local and

does not
occur north-
wards much
beyond the
Caledonian
Canal. It
seems to
affect damp
meadows,
marshy
ground on
the sides of hills, and similar places.

The egg is pale brownish and very glossy. It
is smooth towards the rounded base, but is ribbed
from just before the middle to the top. The eggs
are laid in batches on leaves of Devil's-bit Scabious.

The caterpillar, when full-grown, is black with
a number of minute whitish dots, each bearing a
short black hair ; short black spines are arranged
in rows along the back. The head is black, with
a groove down the front and short hairs on the
sides. The true legs are black, and the false legs
and the under parts of the body are dull rust-
coloured. The caterpillars hatch in June or
July, and towards the end of August they con-
struct silken webs, in which they establish themselves for hibernation. Early in the following
March they recommence feeding. Besides wild
Scabious they will eat Honeysuckle and the garden
kinds of *Scabiosa*.

THE MARSH FRITILLARY

The chrysalis is pale buff, with orange points on the body ; the wing cases are marked with black and orange. It is suspended from a silken web, which is attached to a leaf or drawn-together leaves.

The female butterfly (illustrated) is reddish-orange or bright tawny in colour ; veins black, breaking up the yellowish transverse bands, and there are three or four transverse black lines, not always distinct ; basal area more or less suffused with black. The butterfly is on the wing in May and June. It does not necessarily occur wherever its food-plant is abundant, but Scabious is always found to be present in the haunts of the butterfly. Where the insect occurs in a particular district, a clue to its whereabouts may be obtained by noting the places where the food-plant flourishes. This species is subject to considerable variation in colour, size, and markings, in all localities.

THE GLANVILLE FRITILLARY

Family NYMPHALIDAE   *Melitaea cinxia*

This is a very local species and is now confined to the Isle of Wight, where it seems to
have a preference for the rougher parts of
the under cliff. It is on the wing in May and
June.

The butterfly is bright brownish-orange with
black markings and the female generally is
slightly paler than the male and the markings are
often blurred. There is much variation in these
black markings ; sometimes these are enlarged,
but more often they are much reduced, and the
central one may be completely absent from all the
wings.

The eggs, yellowish-white at first, sometimes
tinged with green, are laid in a cluster on the
under side of the tip of a leaf of the narrow-leaved
Plantain.

The caterpillar, when mature, is black with
white dots, and black bristles arising from
greenish warts. The head is red, and notched on
the crown, and it is distinguished by the red fore
legs. It feeds in early spring on Plantain. When-
ever the caterpillars are met with, it is well to
remember that only the full-grown ones should be

taken, as the smaller ones do not thrive very well in confinement.

The chrysalis is brownish in colour, and is ornamented with orange on the thorax, and with  orange points and black marks on the body. It may be found in April and early May suspended from the lower parts of the stems of the Plantain or other plants nearby.

It is recorded that in the seventeenth century the butterfly was named after a Lady Glanville, who was interested in butterflies, and whose will was disputed on that ground. This fact serves to show that entomology, as a pursuit, was not much thought of at that time, and that those who collected butterflies, were apt to be regarded by their friends as being—well, just a " wee bit daft."

Since 1945 several attempts have been made to introduce this butterfly into other areas, notably the Wirral Peninsula in Cheshire and the New Forest.

THE HEATH FRITILLARY

Family NYMPHALIDAE   *Mellicta athalia*

This species was found in England in the counties of Essex, Kent, Surrey, Devonshire and Cornwall. It is not known to occur in northern England or Scotland. Clearings in woods or their heathy borders are the kind of places this butterfly appears to prefer. It is, unfortunately, becoming scarcer in England than it used to be, and has quite disappeared from some of the districts in which it was formerly common. In Ireland it occurs near Killarney.

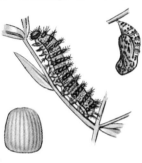

The egg is upright, ribbed, and pale whitish-green in colour, and laid in a cluster usually on a leaf of Cow-wheat. As the caterpillar matures the shell becomes greyish.

The caterpillar, when full-grown, is black on the back, becoming olive tinged on the sides and underneath ; the divisions between the rings are olive. The whole of the upper surface, except a line along the middle, is dotted with white, and there are eleven white-tipped yellowish spines on each ring, except the first and last, which have four spines each ; the third ring has eight, and the second and eleventh have each ten spines. The head is black marked with white, and is clothed with short black hairs. Cow-wheat appears to be the chief food of the caterpillar, but

it has also been found feeding on Foxglove, Plantain, and Woodsage. It hatches from the egg in July, feeds for a few weeks, and then hibernates with others under a web. In April and May it becomes active again, feeds up quickly, and appears as a butterfly in June and early July.

The chrysalis is pale ochreous, the markings on the wing cases are black, and those on the other parts are orange and black.

The male butterfly (illustrated) is brownish-orange, and the markings are black or blackish ; the bases of the wings are clouded with blackish, and the fringes are white checkered with black. There is much variation in this species and the black markings are subject to modification. Sometimes the whole of the wings, with the exception of a series of orange spots, are blackish, and again the ground colour may be pale tawny or deep reddish.

THE RED ADMIRAL BUTTERFLY

Family NYMPHALIDAE   *Vanessa atalanta*

garden
14/3/07

Generally distributed throughout the British Isles it is rarely seen on the wing before the end of May, but June seems to be about the normal time, and continuing onwards to the end of October or even into November. The blossoms of Ivy, Hop, Thistle, etc., are attractive, and in the autumn it is fond of making excursions into the flower garden and orchard, where it takes toll of flower and fruit, an over-ripe pear or plum being its special weakness.

The butterfly will certainly arrest attention by the vivid contrast of black and scarlet, but Nature, ever excellent in her colour schemes, has toned down the glare of the scarlet by the addition of some splashes and dots of white on the fore wings, and some dots of black on the hind wings. There is also a delicate tracing of blue along the outer margin of the fore wings, and a touch of blue at the angle of the hind wings, the scalloped margins

95

of all the wings being white relieved by black points.

The egg, at first, is green but changes to greenish-black as the caterpillar matures, with the ten ribs showing up more or less transparent. It

is laid in an upright position on nettle leaves and young shoots.

The caterpillar is rather variable in colour. Some are blackish, freckled with white, with two yellow stripes on the sides ; others are greyish, marked with yellowish-green. The rows of branched spines are usually yellow, except those nearest the head, which are black or tipped with black. The caterpillars do not live in companies, but each individual constructs for itself a kind of tent by spinning together the leaves of its food-plant, the common Stinging-nettle.

The chrysalis is greyish, ornamented with gold along the centre of the back, and on the thorax and head ; the projections are also tinged with metallic gloss. It is generally suspended under a canopy of nettle leaves.

THE PAINTED LADY BUTTERFLY

Family NYMPHALIDAE   *Vanessa cardui*

This butterfly has been observed, sometimes in abundance, in every part of the British Isles. It is a well-known migrant and its proper home is probably in Northern Africa, where, at times, it becomes so exceedingly numerous that emigration

is possibly a necessity, for it quits the land of its birth in great swarms. Early immigrants may be seen on the wing in this country in May or June, and they continue on the wing each day long after other kinds have retired for the night. They usually occur singly, and seem to become attached to some short stretch of ground, over which they career to and fro with almost mechanical regularity.

The egg, at first green in colour, becomes gradually darker. It is strongly ribbed from the base to the top, where it turns over towards a central hollow ; it is also finely cross-ribbed. It is laid on the leaves of the Thistle, usually only one on a leaf.

The caterpillar has a dark greyish head, covered with short bristles. The body varies from greyish-green to blackish, and the darker colour is generally freckled with pale yellowish. There is a black line along the back, and the lines on the

sides are yellowish. Although Thistles appear
to be the principal food-plant, it has been found
feeding on Mallow, Burdock, and even Nettle.

The chrysalis is grey or greenish, striped or
shaded with brownish. The raised points are
burnished and have a golden effect, as also have
other parts, chiefly on the back.

The butterfly is usually tawny-orange in colour,
but in some specimens there is a tinge of pink ;
the markings are black, and there are some white
spots on the tips of the fore wings. The black
markings on the hind wings are subject to variation in size, and sometimes they run one into the
other. This union of the spots is occasionally
accompanied by a blackish suffusion spreading
more or less over the entire surface of the wings.

THE SMALL TORTOISESHELL BUTTERFLY

Family NYMPHALIDAE *Aglais urticae*

This butterfly is one of the prettiest that we have in this country and is generally distributed. Its reddish-orange colour, marked with yellow patches, black spots and blue crescents, gives it a charming appearance as it rests on a flower with wings fully expanded to the sunlight. When the wings are closed up, however, the butterfly seems to disappear, as the under side is quite sombre in colour.

The ground colour of the wings is subject to modification as regards the shade of red in the orange, and this may be intense or reduced to just a mere tinge. The black markings also vary in size and may be more or less connected or even confluent ; a greater or lesser amount of blackish suffusion on the hind wings generally accompanies confluence of the spots on the fore wings. There are two broods in the year, one in June, the other in August and September. Some of the later brood

THE SMALL TORTOISESHELL
BUTTERFLY

hibernate and reappear in the earliest sunny days of spring. The illustration represents the female.

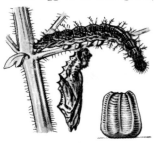

The egg is at first green, but later becomes tinted with yellow and the ribs stand out clear and transparent. The eggs are laid in a cluster on the under side of a terminal leaf of a Nettle plant in May and again in July.

The caterpillar, when full-grown, is yellowish, closely covered with speckling and short hairs ; there is a black line down the centre of the back, bordered on each side by the ground colour. The spiracles are black, ringed with yellow. The yellowish spines have black tips. Head black, hairy, and speckled with yellow. These caterpillars are gregarious from the time they hatch from the egg until the last stage.

The chrysalis is most often of some shade of grey and sometimes tinged with pinkish. The points on the upper parts of the body are in some examples metallic at the base, and occasionally the metallic lustre spreads over the thorax and other parts as well.

THE LARGE TORTOISESHELL BUTTERFLY

Family NYMPHALIDAE   *Nymphalis polychloros*

Lanes margined with trees, especially Elms, or the verges of woods are the most likely places to find this butterfly. It has always been a species restricted to the Midlands and southern England. At present it has a very restricted range in Suffolk and north Essex.

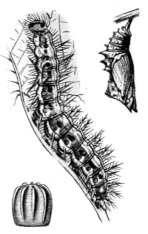

The egg is described as purplish with whitish ribs. The ribs vary from seven to nine.

The caterpillar, in the adult stage, is black, with a speckled dark ochreous band traversed by a black central line on the back; the sides are dappled with ochreous grey; the under parts are brown, dappled with darker and merging into the black. The spines are dark ochreous tipped with black, and the head is shiny black and bristly. The caterpillars live in large companies, often at the top of a high Elm tree. They also may be found on Willow, Sallow, Aspen, Poplar, and various fruit trees, especially Cherry.

The chrysalis is greyish, tinged with reddish, sprinkled with greenish, and shaded with brown

THE LARGE TORTOISESHELL BUTTERFLY

and black ; the back of the body nearest the thorax is adorned with golden spots.

The butterfly is brownish-orange with black spots on the fore wings ; on the front area of the hind wings there is a black spot. Sometimes the black spots of the fore wings are united, forming blotches on the front and inner areas, and the ground colour may be lighter on the fore wings, with the hind wings blacker. The illustration represents the male.

Although this butterfly is often common in the caterpillar state, the perfect insect which emerges in July and August is more frequently seen in the spring after hibernation than before that event. Large numbers of the caterpillars are destroyed by their great enemies, parasitic flies, chiefly *Apanteles*. An observer states that from fifty chrysalids only one butterfly resulted, all the others were found to be filled with parasites.

THE PEACOCK BUTTERFLY

Family NYMPHALIDAE

Inachis io

This butterfly, although not always abundant, is to be, or has been, found in almost every part of the kingdom, becoming scarcer in Scotland. It is on the wing in August and September. Clover fields are attractive, and so also are orchards. It passes the winter in some hollow tree trunk, wood stack, or similar place, and re-appears usually in March or April or occasionally even as early as February.

The butterfly is not likely to be mistaken for any other kind. The brownish-red velvety wings bear its own particular badge, the " peacock eyes." The marks on the hind wings are more like " eyes " than are those of the fore wings, and on these wings the brownish-red is confined to a large patch below the eye-mark, the remainder being blackish, powdered with yellow scales on the basal area. In a state of nature the butterfly seems little given to variation. Usually the

THE PEACOCK BUTTERFLY

Peacock assumes the perfect state but once in a year.

The egg is olive-green in colour and has eight ribs which turn over the top. They are laid in April or May in batches on the upper part of Nettle plants and under the young leaves.

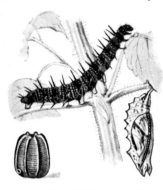

The caterpillar, when mature, is velvety black with white dots. The spines are black and rather glossy and the body is also provided with short hair which gives the velvety appearance. The head is shining black. It usually feeds with others in June and July on the common Stinging Nettle.

When about to pupate the caterpillars usually wander away to some branch or leaf-stalk of a bush or tree, but they have been found under a tent-like arrangement of the lower leaves of Nettle.

The chrysalis may be greenish, greyish, or pale brown, and is usually stippled with blackish. Some of the points have a metallic lustre, especially on the antennae and the outline of the wing cases.

THE CAMBERWELL BEAUTY · BUTTERFLY

Family NYMPHALIDAE   *Nymphalis antiopa*

This beautiful immigrant butterfly is rare in the British Isles, and its appearance has been recorded at long and erratic intervals, in widely separated districts of the country. It visits Ireland occasionally, and in the spring of 1918 several specimens were obtained at Rannoch and other localities in Scotland.

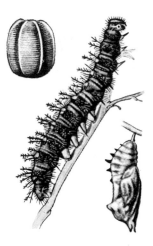

The egg is, at first, deep ochreous-yellow, changing to red-brown, and just before the larva hatches out becoming leaden-grey. The eight or nine ribs are most prominent below the top and disappear before the base is reached. They are laid on twigs or stems in small batches of from 30 or 40 up to larger ones of 150 to 250.

The caterpillar, as described by Mr. Frohawk, is a deep velvety black, densely sprinkled with whitish warts, each emitting a fine white hair. Down the centre of the back is a series of rust-red markings. The head is dull black and hairy, with a deep notch on the crown. The legs are black

THE CAMBERWELL BEAUTY BUTTERFLY

and shining and the four pairs of prolegs are rust colour, and the anal pair are black with pale reddish feet. It will feed on Sallow, Willow, Birch, and Elm. It covers the leaves of its food-plant with a silken web, and lives thereon with others in groups which do not separate until they are ready to prepare for the chrysalis state.

In the chrysalis the dorsal half of the head and wing points are black, and the ventral half orange. The whole surface is finely furrowed. The ground colour is pale buff.

The butterfly is chocolate-brown and the wings are bordered with ochreous, speckled with black scales, and there are blue spots placed on a dark band just before the ochreous border. The butterflies hibernate, and when they leave their winter retreats in the spring, the colour of the border is considerably paler or often even white.

garden. Sept '97 — on sedum

THE COMMA BUTTERFLY

Family NYMPHALIDAE   *Polygonia c-album*

Up to about 1924 this butterfly had been gradually disappearing from all its old localities, and was more or less confined to Herefordshire, Worcestershire, and Monmouthshire. Since then there has been a remarkable increase in its numbers, and it has been reported from the southern, eastern, and midland counties and even the London district.

The butterfly is deep tawny or fulvous with brownish borders and black spots. It is at once recognized by its jagged wing shape and the silver " comma " mark in the middle of the under side of the hind wing. On the under side the wings are various shades of brown, sometimes variegated with yellowish and greenish.

The summer brood of this butterfly produces two forms, typical and var. *hutchinsoni*. The latter being much brighter and yellower, and with the outer margins of the fore wings not so indented and the projections shorter. The illustration represents the male.

The eggs are, at first, green with whitish ribs, but change to yellowish before the caterpillars

THE COMMA BUTTERFLY

hatch out. They are usually laid in chains of three or four.

The caterpillar, when full-grown, is black, netted with greyish; the spines on the second to fifth rings are yellowish, and those on the other

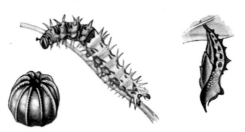

rings are white; the back from ring 6 to ring 10 is broadly white, marked with black, and the other rings are more or less yellowish. The head is black and the crown is lobed, with two short club-like knobs. The usual food-plants of the caterpillars are Hop, Nettle, and Currant, with possibly Gooseberry and Elm.

The chrysalis is brownish; there is a greyish line along the back of the body, and a brownish stripe along the spiracles; there are also some silvery and golden spots.

THE PURPLE EMPEROR BUTTERFLY

Family NYMPHALIDAE   *Apatura iris*

Although this beautiful butterfly is certainly
not so common as in former times, it still occurs
in the larger woods of most of the midland,
western, and southern counties of England. It
will be found on the wing in July, flying amongst

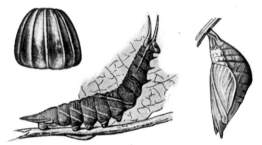

the trees, usually resting on a leaf of the higher
branches.

The eggs are pale olive-green and cylindrical in
shape ; they have about fourteen ribs. They
may be looked for in August on the upper surface
of a leaf of the Sallow.

The caterpillar, when full-grown, is green,
merging into yellowish towards the anal points
(tails) ; the oblique stripes on the sides are
yellowish, edged with reddish. The head and
the two horn-like projections are reddish-grey
and covered with warts and bristles.

The chrysalis is whitish, tinged with green ;
the oblique lines and the veins of the wings are
whitish. The caterpillar spins a mat of silk to
the under side of a Sallow leaf and the chrysalis

THE PURPLE EMPEROR BUTTERFLY

is suspended by the claspers from the silken mat.

On account of its large size and the beautiful purple sheen over its brownish-black velvety wings, this butterfly is always counted a prize by the collector. It is, however, only the male (illustrated) that dons the purple, and he only when seen from the proper angle. The female is without the purple and her wings are browner; the white spots and bands are rather wider than those of the male. On the hind wings of both sexes there is a black spot ringed with tawny, which is sometimes centred with white.

THE WHITE ADMIRAL BUTTERFLY

Family NYMPHALIDAE   *Ladoga camilla*

This species was formerly restricted to the southern and eastern counties of England. Of recent years, however, this butterfly has been extending its range. In the New Forest, Hampshire, it is often abundant in July, and almost all writers on our butterflies have commented on the graceful flight of the White Admiral, as it skims high and low through the woodland glades.

The butterfly has blackish wings with large white spots and bands, somewhat similar to those of the Purple Emperor. The under side of the wings is most beautifully ornamented. The illustration represents the female.

The egg is described as olive-green in colour, and of the shape of an orange, but flatter at the base and top. It is laid in July and is stated to hatch in about fourteen days.

The caterpillar, when full-grown, is green, darker on the back and lighter on the sides, roughened with yellow dots. There is a yellow-marked white line above the feet. The spines are reddish. The head is brownish and set with short spines, which are inclined backwards. In the autumn, when quite small, it constructs a winter retreat by fastening a growing leaf of honeysuckle to a twig with silken threads, and then with more silk, it draws the edges of the leaf together, and so forms a secure chamber where it rests until the following spring.

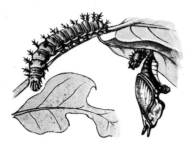

The chrysalis is of remarkable shape. It is brownish, with a purplish or olive tinge ; behind the rounded hump there is a patch of bright green, and above the wing cases a beautiful golden sheen. There are also other metallic spots on various parts. Altogether it is one of the prettiest of British butterfly chrysalids.

THE DUKE OF BURGUNDY FRITILLARY

Family NEMEOBIIDAE   *Hamearis lucina*

This butterfly appears to be widely distributed, although to a certain extent local, throughout England, and is, perhaps, rather more common in the south. It has occurred at Dumfries in Scotland. It is a woodland species, and prefers the sunny glades, and also resorts to the broader rides and pathways.

The egg, when laid, is very glassy in appearance, but it gradually turns to a pinkish-grey ; and when the caterpillar is formed inside, the shell becomes transparent, and its occupant can be clearly seen. When the young caterpillar makes its exit, it eats a considerable portion of its shell, and afterwards consumes the remainder. The eggs are to be found at the end of May on the under side of the leaves of the Cowslip.

The caterpillar, when in its last skin, is brown, covered with short whitish hairs, among which are some dark brown or blackish hairs ; the lines on the back and sides are blackish, and there are black dots on each segment. Head, brown, notched on the crown ; eyes and jaws brownish. It feeds from June to August on Cowslip or Primrose, and hides among dead and withered leaves beneath the food-plant.

THE DUKE OF BURGUNDY FRITILLARY

The chrysalis is pale whity-brown, hairy above, with black dots ; head and upper edge of the wing cases streaked with black.

The male butterfly (illustrated) is blackish, with three transverse tawny bands on the fore wings ; these are crossed by the black veins, and so form a series of irregular spots. Those on the outer margin have black centres ; on the hind wings there are three or four tawny spots, and a series of black centred tawny spots on the outer area. The female is similar to the male, but the tawny markings are wider, and the wings are always broader and the apex of the fore wings is not so distinctly pointed. Occasionally a few butterflies emerge in August, or later, but they usually remain in the chrysalis until May or June.

THE LONG-TAILED BLUE BUTTERFLY

Family LYCAENIDAE *Lampides boeticus*

The occurrence of this butterfly in England is exceedingly infrequent. It is believed to be migratory in its habits, and it is supposed that the occasional specimens that arrive in this country come to us by way of the west coast of Europe. Isolated specimens have been taken from time to time in the past, principally in the southern counties of England. The species is common in Africa and in Southern Europe. In its proper home there is a succession of broods of the butterfly, and if by chance a few females were to visit this country in the early summer, they would most probably lay eggs, and the caterpillars resulting would be able to feed up, and attain the perfect state here.

The butterfly is purplish-blue suffused with fuscous, especially on all margins, except the inner one; there are two velvety black spots, encircled with pale blue at the anal angle of the hind wings, and a slender black tail, tipped with white which appears to be a continuation of vein 2. The male is slightly smaller than the female and very similar in coloration and form.

The caterpillar is described as being green to olive in colour, with a dark stripe on the back, double oblique lines on the sides, and a yellowish line below the flesh-coloured spiracles ; the head is amber-brown. It feeds upon the green seeds in pods of the Pea Family, including the garden Pea and the Lupin.

The chrysalis is of a red or yellowish colour, and dotted with brown. It has a silken girdle and is said to be attached to a stem, but more often, probably, it is fixed up among the withered leaves of the food-plant.

THE SMALL BLUE BUTTERFLY

Family LYCAENIDAE   *Cupido minimus*

The haunts of this species are warm and sunny grassy hollows and slopes, and it is often common on the chalk hills of the southern counties of England, from the end of May to the end of June. Widely distributed but local in the midlands and

western counties where chalk or limestone is found ; also in restricted localities farther north, extending as far as Aberdeen. It is much more plentiful in Ireland, especially on the limestone of the west and on the coast hills near Belfast, and even frequents the sandhills of the Dublin coast.

The egg is pale greenish in colour, netted with whitish ; it is laid in June on the calyx of a flower-bud, generally low down, of the Kidney Vetch.

The caterpillar, when full-grown, is brownish, sometimes tinged with pink. The fine bristles are dark brown ; there is a darker line along the middle of the back, and a line of dark marks on each side. The head is black and shining.

Although the caterpillars feed up rather quickly, yet when full-grown and apparently ready to assume the chrysalis state, they do not effect the change until the following May or June, so it will be seen that this species continues the caterpillar existence for something over ten months.

THE SMALL BLUE BUTTERFLY

The chrysalis is described as whitish-grey, approaching to drab, palest on the back, greyish on the head and thorax, both of which are marked with a black dorsal stripe. On either side there is a row of short black dashes and the pale ground colour is sprinkled with very minute black specks. It is attached head upwards to a stem or a blade of grass.

The butterfly, sometimes referred to as the " Bedford Blue " and also as the " Little Blue," is blackish or sooty-brown in both sexes, but the male is powdered, more or less, with silvery-blue scales. The under side, in great contrast to the upper side, is greyish-white with a tinge of blue at the base of each wing, but chiefly on the hind pair ; the spots are black encircled with white.

THE SHORT-TAILED BLUE BUTTERFLY

Family LYCAENIDAE   *Everes argiades*

This butterfly, known also as the " Bloxworth Blue," was not known to occur in Britain until 1885 when a male and a female specimen were captured at Bloxworth Heath in Dorset. Since that time it has only been recorded in England at long intervals and in widely separated districts. No doubt those localities from which specimens were taken have been closely investigated during recent years, but no further captures have been recorded. This seems to indicate that it is not really indigenous, but that its presence is possibly due to accidental introduction or migration.

The male butterfly (illustrated) is violet-blue with the veins rather darker ; the outer margin is narrowly bordered with blackish, and there are some black dots on the outer margin of the hind wings ; the fringes are white, and there is a short and slender tail on the hind wings. The female is brownish, tinged with violet towards the base ; the tails are slightly longer than those of the male.

The following details of the early stages are obtained from Mr. Frohawk's life-history of the species.

The egg is a pale greenish-blue, but varies both in colour and the structure of the reticulations, which are white, resembling frosted glass.

The caterpillars were hatched from eggs that

were laid in the South of France, and were reared on Bird's-foot Trefoil, of which they ate the flowers, seeds, and leaves. When full-grown it is   of the usual wood-louse shape and the ground colour is pale green ; the whole of the back is densely studded with short whitish or brownish bristles. There is a dark green stripe along the centre of the back, and pale green oblique stripes on the sides. The head is black and shining, and is hidden under the first ring when the caterpillar is not feeding or moving about.

The chrysalis is pale green and finely reticulated ; the wing cases are rather lighter green, and the veins are white ; there is a blackish line along the centre of the back. The whole surface, except the wings, is sprinkled with slightly curved and moderately long white hairs. It is attached to the food-plant by a silk pad at the tail, and a thread round the body. The butterfly emerges in about ten to fourteen days, according to temperature.

THE SILVER-STUDDED BLUE BUTTERFLY

Family LYCAENIDAE   *Plebejus argus*

This butterfly ranges through the greater part of England and Wales, and into Scotland as far as Perthshire. It is more often found on sandy heaths, and especially, in some years, in the heather-clad districts of Surrey and Hampshire,

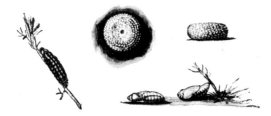

as well as other counties in England. It is on the wing in June, July, and August.

The egg, Mr. Frohawk states, resembles white porcelain, both in colour and texture, and is deposited singly, and adheres firmly to the receptacle.

Caterpillars hatched out early in April, from eggs laid the previous summer, and they were reared on Gorse. When full-grown they were reddish-brown in colour, finely dotted with white, and from each dot a tiny hair arose ; the stripe on the back and line on the side were black, edged with white ; the head black and shining. Another food-plant is Bird's-foot Vetch.

The chrysalis has a pale brownish and shining head ; body brown with a darker line on the back ; wing cases and thorax a dull yellowish-green.

THE SILVER-STUDDED BLUE
BUTTERFLY

The male of this butterfly (right wing) is purplish-blue, with a black border on the outer margins, and sometimes black dots on the hind wings. The colour varies in shade, and occasionally may be of a lilac tint, and the border varies in width, sometimes reduced to a mere line. The female is sooty-brown, powdered with blue scales on the basal area ; there is generally a series of orange marks forming a more or less complete band on the outer margin of the hind wings. The under side is bluish-grey in the male, and brownish-grey in the female ; the black spots are ringed with white, and there is a black-edged orange band on all the wings. There is a good deal of variation of the black spots as regards size and shape.

In a general way the male is rather larger than the female, but this is not always so.

THE BROWN ARGUS BUTTERFLY

Family LYCAENIDAE   *Aricia agestis*

This species is widely distributed throughout
the southern half of England, and also in Wales.
It is more or less common in some parts of Derby-
shire, Yorkshire, and Lancashire. The ordinary
form of the butterfly is on the wing in May and
June and again in August. Although chiefly
associated with Rock-rose, especially in chalky
districts, it occurs, too, among Hemlock Stork's-
bill, upon which plant the caterpillar also
feeds.

The butterfly is sooty-brown on the fore wings,
and a row of reddish-orange spots on the outer
margin of all the wings ; the fringes are white.
The under side is greyish-brown and the black
spots are distinctly ringed with white. The
female (illustrated) has larger orange markings
than the male, and the outline of the fore wings is
rather rounder on the outer margin.

The orange spots referred to in the male are
sometimes absent, and in this respect lead up to
the form known as the Durham Argus, var.
salmacis, which is blackish above and ochreous-
brown below ; the black spots are much smaller
and some may be absent altogether. The male
has a black discal spot and the female a white one
on the upper side of the fore wings. The hind
wings have a red or orange band on both surfaces

THE BROWN ARGUS BUTTERFLY

In Scotland both sexes have a conspicuous white discal spot on the fore wings, and the spots on the under side are white, rarely centred with black. This form is known as the Scotch White Spot, var. *artaxerxes*.

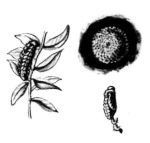

The egg, which is whitish, is laid on the upper side of a young leaf of the Rock-rose.

The caterpillar has a black shining head; the body is green with whitish hairs, a pinkish line along the back, a whitish one along the sides; the green colour becomes dingy as the caterpillar matures. Caterpillars from the first brood may be found in July, and those from the second brood hibernate and feed up in April.

The chrysalis is obscure yellowish-green, the front of the thorax is edged with pinkish, and there are bands of the same colour on the back and sides of the body; the thorax and wing cases are rather glossy. It is held in position, between the leaves of the food-plant, by a few silken threads. This species is double-brooded in the south, but the northern races occur as a single brood. Recent evidence suggests that the northern forms belong to a distinct species, *Aricia allous*, well-known in northern Europe.

THE COMMON BLUE BUTTERFLY

Family LYCAENIDAE   *Polyommatus icarus*

This butterfly is to be found almost everywhere in the country, and its distribution extends throughout the United Kingdom, except perhaps the Shetland Isles. In England there are two broods, and in some years probably three in the

southern counties. It may be seen on the wing all through the season from May to September.

The egg is whitish-green in colour, netted with glossy white, and is usually laid on the upper side of a terminal leaf of the Bird's-foot Trefoil or on Rest-Harrow.

The caterpillar is green, covered with short, brownish hairs, with which are mixed some longer ones ; it is wrinkled on the side, ridged on the back, and the line along the middle of the back is darker. Head black and glossy. The plants mentioned above are known to be the food of the caterpillar, but eggs have also been found, in Scotland, on Red Clover, Plantain, Burnet Saxifrage, and Yarrow. Those feeding on Rest-Harrow seem to prefer the blossom. They are to be found, after hibernation, in April, and a second brood in June and July.

The chrysalis is green, with the head, wing

cases, and sometimes the hinder part of the body, tinged with buff. It is placed in a loose cocoon formed of a few threads of silk among the stems of the food-plant.

The male butterfly (right wing) is blue, with either a tinge of violet or mauve. There is a narrow edge of black on the outer margins of all the wings; the veins are generally pale blue, sometimes becoming blackish towards the outer margins. The female is most often brown, with some blue scales on the basal area of all the wings; there is a series of orange crescents before a row of black spots on the outer margin; the hind wings have an outer row of black spots, edged outwardly with white, and inwardly with orange. There is a good deal of variation, especially in the female, and quite a number of gynandrous specimens have been recorded, some of them being male on the right side and female on the left, in others the reverse was the case.

THE CHALKHILL BLUE BUTTERFLY

Family LYCAENIDAE   *Lysandra coridon*

This species is often abundant in July and August, chiefly the latter month, on chalk downs in the southern counties of England.

The butterfly is fairly constant in the matter of colour. Silvery-blue perhaps best expresses the general colour of the male (right wing); sometimes very pale, and sometimes tinged with greenish. The blackish border on the outer margin of the fore wings varies in width and intensity. The black border on the hind wings is often narrow, but sometimes broad. The fringes are white chequered with blackish on the fore wings, but with seeming continuation of the veins through those of the hind wings. The female is sooty-brown above ; the fringes are white, chequered with brown, and those of the fore wings are tinged with brown. There are generally some blue scales at the base of the fore wings, and over a larger portion of the basal area and occasionally over the whole discal area of the hind wings.

The egg is flat on the top, with a slightly darker pit (the micropyle) in the centre ; the sides are rounded, netted, and studded, and the colour is

whitish-green. It is laid during July and August
on the stems of the usual stunted herbage to be

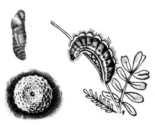

found growing on
chalk downs, and is
deposited singly.

The caterpillars
do not hatch out
until the following
spring. When full-
grown they are
bright green in
colour with light
brown hairs. Other-
wise they resemble closely the caterpillars of the
Adonis Blue. The food-plant is the Horseshoe
Vetch.

The chrysalis is ochreous-yellow, the thorax and
wing cases rather glossy and the body is slightly
hairy. It is placed on the ground at the base of
the food-plant.

The species is subject to a considerable range
of variation on the under side. Very striking
aberrations are sometimes obtained.

THE ADONIS BLUE BUTTERFLY

Family LYCAENIDAE   *Lysandra bellargus*

Although this butterfly is found in similar situations as the Chalkhill Blue, it is more local, and found mostly in the counties of Kent, Surrey, and Sussex. It is, however, rather common at Ventnor, and in some other parts of the Isle of Wight, and is also found along the south coast, westward as far as Devon.

The egg is greenish-white, becoming greener in tint towards the top, which is depressed ; the netting is whitish and shining, and somewhat rougher on the sides.

The caterpillar, when full-grown, is described as deep green in colour, covered with tiny black speckles, bearing little black bristles ; on the top of each of the eight pairs of dorsal humps is a bright yellow dash, and these dashes form in effect two yellow stripes, interrupted by the deeply sunk divisions ; the line along the back is darker than the ground colour, and the spiracles are black. The head is dark brown, and there are two yellow dots on the first ring of the body. The food-plant is the Horseshoe Vetch.

The chrysalis at first is greenish-brown with greenish wing cases, the whole afterwards becomes ochreous ; the body is slightly hairy. It is placed on or just under the surface in a frail cocoon, consisting of a few silk threads.

THE ADONIS BLUE BUTTERFLY

The male butterfly (right wing) is of a bright blue colour, but is not quite constant in tint. In some specimens there is a distinct mauve shade, and in others the blue may be tinged with greenish. The veins become distinctly black on the outer margins. The female is dark brown, sometimes slaty-black, with orange spots on the outer margins ; there is a black spot on the fore wings, and the fringes of all the wings are white, chequered with black.

This species is subject to almost as much variation as the Chalkhill Blue.

From eggs laid in August, the caterpillars hatch towards the end of September. Butterflies from these caterpillars are on the wing between mid-May and mid-June, thus occupying about nine months in passing through the various stages from egg to perfect insect. From eggs laid in May and June, the butterflies appear in August and September.

THE MAZARINE BLUE BUTTERFLY

Family LYCAENIDAE   *Cyaniris semiargus*

An extremely rare species in England, and records of over a hundred years ago show that it was, even then, very scarce and local. It was chiefly found in the chalky districts of the southern midlands and occasionally in the southern counties. Appearing fitfully and at long intervals since it was first reported as far back as 1828, it was recorded as being taken about forty-five years ago in Kent, but it has not since been seen in that county. A male specimen was recorded in June, 1908, as being taken at Mortimer in Berkshire. It occurs in May and June, and again in July and August, over the greater part of Europe, and its range extends eastwards as far as Siberia and Mongolia.

The male butterfly (illustrated) is a dull purplish-blue, narrowly bordered with blackish on the outer margins ; the female is dark brown. On the under side both sexes are pale greyish-brown, with a bluish tinge at the base ; there is a black discal spot, and a series of black spots beyond, all ringed with white.

The egg is described as pale blue-green in colour, small and round in shape, and covered

THE MAZARINE BLUE BUTTERFLY

with a beautiful reticulated network pattern like
white frosted glass.

The caterpillar is a dingy yellowish-green, with
darker lines on the back and sides ; there are fine
hairs on the body, and the head and spiracles are
dark brown. It feeds in July and August and
again in the spring after hibernation on the
flowers and seeds of Thrift, Kidney Vetch,
Clover, and Melilot.

The chrysalis is rather oval in shape, pale olive-
green when first formed in September, but olive-
brown later ; it is attached by the tail to a stalk of
the food-plant and has a silken girdle.

THE LARGE BLUE BUTTERFLY

Family LYCAENIDAE   *Maculinea arion*

This species is the largest " Blue " found in
this country. It is very rare and fitful in its
appearance, isolated specimens having been taken
in the past in widely separated districts. It is
now chiefly to be found in north Cornwall. We
are indebted to Mr. Frohawk for the following
details :

The egg is bluish-white, and is laid singly
among the buds of Wild Thyme.

The caterpillar, whose life-history is one of
the most remarkable known, resembles, in its
colouring, the flower-buds of the Thyme. After
the third moult, the colour is a dull, ochreous-
pink and there are four rows of long curved hairs.
The head is ochreous, with dark brown markings.

THE LARGE BLUE BUTTERFLY

When the third moult is complete, the caterpillar rests for a time and then starts wandering
about. It loses its foothold and falls to the ground
and perhaps will wander for some hours. Then
a passing ant may find it and begins caressing it

with its antennae. These *arion* caterpillars have
a gland on the tenth segment which exudes a
liquid which the ants like. The ant leaves the
caterpillar at intervals returning each time to
caress and milk it. The " courtship " often lasts
for an hour or more. Finally, by some mystic
sense, the caterpillar prepares itself to be carried
off by the ant. It hunches its back and the ant
seizes it and carries it to the ants' nest, descending
with it to the brood chamber. The caterpillar
then enters into its new existence and partakes of
its first meal of a strange new food—*i.e.* an ant
larva of very small size.

For the following six weeks it feeds and grows
rapidly until it has trebled itself in size and
become vastly different in appearance. As winter
approaches it settles down for hibernation in a
cavity in the nest. In the spring it awakens from
its long winter sleep and feeds again on its strange
food.

When ready to turn to a chrysalis, it attaches
itself to the roof, by its anal claspers, to a pad of
silk. The effort of changing causes it to fall to

THE LARGE BLUE BUTTERFLY

the bottom of the chamber. After about twenty-one days the imago emerges and finds its way through the passages of the ants' nests to the outer world, where, as a perfect butterfly, it climbs a stem and dries its wings.

The chrysalis, when first formed, is ochreous but becomes darker gradually.

The butterfly, on the upper side, is deep blue, and the outer margins of all the wings are bordered with blackish; the spots are black; the hind wings have a row of black dots on the outer margin, and sometimes, especially in the female where there is usually a series of black dots just beyond the central area. The fringes are white. The under side is greyish, tinged with blue towards the base of each wing.

The chief variation is in the number and size of the spots; a dwarf form is stated to occur at times in all localities.

The Conservation of Wild Creatures and Wild Plants Act 1975 makes it illegal, except under licence from the Nature Conservancy Council or in a few other specified circumstances, to kill, injure or take, or to have in your possession the Large Blue butterfly, or to sell a specimen even when dead.

THE HOLLY BLUE BUTTERFLY

Family LYCAENIDAE   *Celastrina argiolus*

This butterfly is widely distributed, and often common, over the whole of the southern counties of England and Wales. North of the Midlands, as well as in Ireland, it is more local, and possibly occurs only in the first brood. It is generally double brooded and sometimes even produces a third brood.

The male butterfly (right wing) is a pretty lilac-tinged blue, with a narrow black edging on the outer margin of the fore wings, often only in evidence towards the tip. The white fringes of the fore wings are distinctly marked with black at the ends of the veins. The female is of the same shade of blue, or sometimes much paler, with a broad blackish border on the outer margin of the fore wings, and varying in width ; there is a series of black dots on the outer margin of the wings. The under side is bluish-white, with an arrangement of black spots, which are subject to slight modification in the matters of size and shape. Butterflies of the first brood are usually to be seen in April and May, and the second in July and August.

The egg is described as whitish or bluish-green

THE HOLLY BLUE BUTTERFLY

in colour. Normally the eggs of the spring butterflies are laid on the under side of the calyces of the flower-buds of Holly, Dogwood, Buckthorn, etc. The second brood eggs are generally laid on Ivy.

The caterpillar, when full-grown, has a blackish head, and the body is bright yellowish-green, with paler lines ; the whole skin of the body is velvety, and thickly covered with yellowish granules, each bearing a minute white hair.

The chrysalis is pale brownish-ochreous, with a thin blackish-brown line on the back of the brown freckled thorax ; the body is marked with rather blotchy arrow-head dashes, and some larger dark brown blotches ; the wing cases are pale greyish, freckled and outlined with brown, and their surface is smooth and glistening ; the other parts are thickly studded with fine, short brownish bristles. It is attached by a fine silk girdle round the waist.

THE SMALL COPPER BUTTERFLY

Family LYCAENIDAE   *Lycaena phlaeas*

This species occurs throughout Britain as far
north as the Orkney Isles. It is very active
and frequents all kinds of open situations, and is
fond of basking
upon flowers,
more particu-
larly those of the
Daisy family,
from which van-
tage ground it
has the habit of
dashing, with
great alertness,
at any other
small butterfly that may happen to fly that way, to
indulge in a playful gambol, after which one may
dart off pursued by the other, both moving so
rapidly that their course is difficult to follow.

The egg is of a yellowish-white colour at first,
and afterwards becomes greyish ; the pattern on
the shell, which resembles network is always
whiter.

The caterpillar is green and similar in tint to
the leaf of Dock or Sorrel upon which it feeds.
It is clothed with short greyish hair which arises
from white dots ; the dorsal line is brownish-
olive, and the ring divisions are well defined.
Head very small, pale brownish, marked with
blackish, and drawn into the first ring of the body
when resting. The legs and prolegs are tinged
with pink, and sometimes the body is marked
with pink.

The chrysalis is pale brown, sometimes tinged
with greenish, and freckled with darker brown ;

THE SMALL COPPER BUTTERFLY

a dark line along the thorax and body, and the wing cases are streaked with blackish ; the body is dotted with black. It is attached to a leaf or stem by the tail, with loose silken threads around the body.

The butterfly is of a coppery-orange colour, spotted with black on the fore wings, the outer series of six spots forming a very irregular row ; the hind wings are blackish, with a wavy orange-red band on the outer margin.

There is considerable variation in this species. Specimens much suffused with blackish sometimes occur. The colour of the hind wings is sometimes steely-grey ; the band on the outer area varies in width a good deal, and may be more or less obscured by the blackish ground colour. The arrangement, size, and shape of the black spots is also subject to much vagary.

THE LARGE COPPER BUTTERFLY

Family LYCAENIDAE   *Lycaena dispar*

Records of over a hundred years ago, show that this brilliant butterfly then occurred in great profusion in the fenny counties of Cambridge and Huntingdon, with the neighbouring ones of Suffolk and Norfolk. It became extinct in Britain in 1851 but can still be found on the Continent, particularly in Holland.

The female butterfly generally is described as of a bright coppery-orange colour, conspicuously marked with black. There are two, sometimes three, spots in the cell of the fore wings, and a series of seven or eight beyond ; the outer margin is broadly marked with black. The hind wings have a black spot in the cell, and a series of black spots beyond, but the basal three-fourths of these wings is often deeply suffused with blackish ; the outer margin is bordered and spotted with black. The under side of the hind wings is of a beautiful silvery blue dotted with black, and has a broad orange band towards the outer margin.

The egg is laid on the leaves of the Great Water Dock, during the month of August, and the young caterpillars emerge in about fourteen days.

THE LARGE COPPER BUTTERFLY

The caterpillar is green, scarcely distinguishable from the colour of the Dock leaf. It feeds until about the end of September, when it retires for hibernation in the old Dock leaves.

It appears again in April and is full-fed in June, and then lies flat on the dock leaf, rarely moving from place to place, and, when it does so, gliding with a slug-like motion, the legs and claspers being entirely concealed. The head is extremely small, and can be completely withdrawn into the second segment.

The chrysalis is obese, blunt at both ends, and is of an ochreous colour. It is suspended by minute hooks at the caudal extremity, and also by a belt round the waist to the under side of a Dock leaf or to a reed stem.

In recent years the Dutch race of this species has been introduced and thrives in one or two localities in East Anglia. This Dutch race is, perhaps, not so fine as the original native English one, but is nevertheless an elegant species to have breeding in this country.

THE GREEN HAIRSTREAK BUTTERFLY

Family LYCAENIDAE   *Callophrys rubi*

This species seems to be pretty generally distributed throughout the British Isles, but is rather more local in Ireland than elsewhere, and it has not yet been reported from the Orkney or Shetland Isles. May and June are the months for the

butterfly on the outskirts of woods, high hedgerows, and boggy heaths. Its resemblance, on the under side, to the leaves on which it rests, is so perfect that it is extremely difficult to see.

The egg is greenish, reticulated with whitish-green; the reticulation is rough on the side, but becomes finer towards and on the top, which has the centre hollowed. It is laid on the petals of the common Furze, in the flower heads of the Bird's-foot Trefoil, or on leaves of the Rock-rose.

The caterpillar feeds in June and July. It is pale green, with a darker line along the back, and yellow oblique stripes on the sides. Among the plants that it has been found upon, or is known to eat, are Dyer's Greenwood, Needle Furze, Broom, Whortleberry; also the berries of Buckthorn, buds of Bramble and Dogwood.

The chrysalis is purplish-brown speckled with black. It is clothed with tiny hairs. It is placed on the ground and has a few strands of silk around and about it.

Both sexes of the butterfly are brown, with a faint golden tinge on the upper side, and green on the under side. The male has a dark, or, when the plumules are dislodged, pale sexual mark, which is oval in shape, and placed at the upper corner of the discal cell in the fore wings. Occasionally there are some orange scales at the anal angle of the hind wings, and more rarely, and in the female usually only at the extremities of veins two and three also. Although generally greenish on the under side of the hind wings, now and then, they are found to be brown in colour, and this change has been ascribed to the action of moisture. On some specimens there is a series of white dots across all the wings on the under side which may be confined to the hind wings only.

THE BROWN HAIRSTREAK BUTTERFLY

Family LYCAENIDAE   *Thecla betulae*

This butterfly has always been considered a local species, appearing to frequent hedgerows occasionally, although its haunts generally are open grounds near woods, where Blackthorn or Sloe is plentiful. It is on the wing in August and September. When seen it is generally high up on, or around, some oak tree. Occasionally, however, it visits the Bramble blossoms. It is generally distributed in southern England and Wales and has occasionally been noted as far north as Cumbria. Its status in Ireland at the present time is uncertain, though there are old records from the south-west of the country.

The male butterfly is blackish-brown, and there is a conspicuous black bar on the fore wings, followed by a pale cloud ; there are two orange marks at the anal angle of the hind wings. The female (illustrated) is blackish-brown and has the black bar, and an orange band beyond ; there are usually three, sometimes two, orange marks on the hind wings at the anal angle. The under side of the male is ochreous, but that of the female is more orange. On the fore wings there is a white-edged streak, and on the hind wings there are two white irregular lines, and the space between them is brownish. Variation is not of a very striking character.

The egg is described as a depressed sphere and white. It is attached to the twigs of Blackthorn in the autumn, often as late as the end of September or beginning of October ; it does not hatch until the spring.

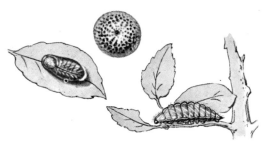

The caterpillar is bright pale green, and the lines on the back and sides are yellowish, as also are the oblique streaks on the sides. There are some bristles along the ridge on the back, and also on that above the feet. It feeds on Blackthorn in May and June, and will eat the foliage of any kind of plum.

The chrysalis is pale reddish-brown, with a dark line down the middle of the back, and some pale oblique streaks on each side ; the wing cases are freckled with darker brown. It pupates on stems or under leaves of the food-plant, close to the ground.

THE PURPLE HAIRSTREAK BUTTERFLY

Family LYCAENIDAE *Quercusia quercus*

This butterfly is generally distributed in all parts of England and Wales, and in Scotland as far north as Ross. In Ireland it has only been recorded from the east and south. It frequents Oak woods, or their borders, in July and August.

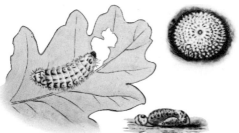

It has a habit of flying around the upper branches of the trees, and is more easy to see than to capture. Occasionally it resorts to lower growing Aspens, probably to feast on the honey-dew, with which the leaves are often covered in hot summers.

The egg is pale brown, tinged with pink, and over this is a whitish network

The caterpillar is reddish-brown and downy; a black line along the back has a whitish edge, and there are whitish oblique stripes, with blackish edge, on each side of the central line; the segments are well marked, and the spiracles are blackish with pale rings. The head, when the caterpillar is resting, is hidden within the first ring of the body, and is brownish and glossy. There is a greyish shield-like mark on the second ring.

The chrysalis is red-brown, with darker freckles ; the body is downy, and there are traces of oblique marks. It does not appear to be fastened by the tail, but the cast larval skin remains attached ; there are a few strands of silk, and, although flimsy, they are sufficient to hold it in position on the ground.

The male butterfly is strongly tinged with purplish-blue, and the veins are blackish ; the outer margins of all the wings are bordered with black. The female (illustrated) is purplish-black, with two patches of bluish-purple in the discal cell and space below ; often there is a similar patch of the same colour between them, the whole forming a large blotch interrupted by the blackish veins. The under side is greyish, with blackish shaded white lines ; a black spot on the anal angle of the hind wings, and a black centred orange spot between veins two and three. Variation in this species is rather exceptional.

THE WHITE-LETTER HAIRSTREAK BUTTERFLY

Family LYCAENIDAE   *Strymonidia w-album*

This species is local, but, as a rule, plentiful enough in its localities. It favours the southern and midland counties of England, scarce in some and more abundant in others. Its northern limit appears to be round about Doncaster and elsewhere in Yorkshire. It is on the wing in July, and usually disports itself around the Elm trees, but is fond of Bramble blossom, and may often be seen feasting on those flowers.

The male butterfly is blackish, with a small whitish sex mark on the fore wing; there is a small orange spot at the anal angle of the hind wings. The female (illustrated) agrees in colour with the male, but the tails are longer, and there is no sex mark on the fore wings. The under side is brownish, with a white line on each wing, that on the hind wings forming a W before the inner margin; the hind wings have a black-edged orange band on the outer margin. The white lines on the under side may be rather broad or very narrow, and that on the hind wings is sometimes so broken up that the W character disappears.

The egg is of a button-like shape, colour sea-

THE WHITE-LETTER HAIRSTREAK
BUTTERFLY

green when first laid, becoming darker later
(Frohawk). It is laid on Elm in July, and remains
thereon throughout the winter.

The caterpillar, when full-grown, is yellowish-
green and covered with short hairs; the ridges of

the back are yellowish, and there are oblique
whitish streaks on each side. The head is black.
When ready to assume the chrysalis state, the
whole body becomes purplish-brown. It feeds
on Wych-elm, but it will eat the leaves of the
Common Elm, and may be obtained in May and
June by beating Wych-elms in localities where the
butterfly is known to occur.

The chrysalis is brownish, sometimes tinged
with purple; covered with tiny bristles, except
on the blackish wing cases, and there are two
purplish lines on the back. It is attached by the
tail, and has a strand or two of silk around it,
generally on the under side of a leaf.

THE BLACK HAIRSTREAK BUTTERFLY

Family LYCAENIDAE   *Strymonidia pruni*

This butterfly seems to be confined, so far as Britain is concerned, to three or four of the midland counties, in wooded districts. It is fond of resting on the flowers of Privet and of the Way-faring-tree. Its time of emergence is very

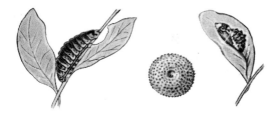

variable, apparently regulated by the vagaries of spring ; generally appearing about the middle of June to early in July.

The eggs are reddish-brown and rather shiny. They are laid in July on the twigs of Blackthorn, but the caterpillars do not hatch out until the following spring.

The caterpillar is described as yellowish-green in colour, with a darker green furrow and purplish ridges along the back ; the ridges are edged with whitish, and the divisions between the rings are yellowish. The head is pale brown. It feeds on the Blackthorn in a state of nature, but will eat leaves of Damson in confinement. It may be obtained in May, in its particular haunts, by beating Sloe bushes into a beating tray, or an inverted open umbrella.

The chrysalis is black, marked on the head and

U

body with yellowish-white. It is attached to the leaf by the tail, and has a silken thread around it.

The butterfly is dark brown or, when quite fresh, brownish-black; there are some orange marks on the outer margin of the hind wings, and these are most distinct in the female in which sex there are generally orange spots on the fore wings also. The male has a pale sexual mark at the end of the cell of the fore wings. The under side is brown, with a bluish-white interrupted line on each wing. All the wings have an orange band on the outer margin, but on the fore wings of the male this is often indistinct; there are some white-edged black spots before it, and, on the hind wings, beyond it also.

THE WOOD WHITE BUTTERFLY

Family PIERIDAE   *Leptidea sinapis*

This fragile-looking little butterfly is somewhat local, but in its particular haunts not altogether uncommon. It is fond of the shady rides and margins of woods, settling on the under side of a leaf on dull or wet days. The first brood is on the wing in May, and the second, when it occurs, in July and August. It is found in many parts of England and Wales, especially in the southern and western counties. Formerly its distribution extended into Cumberland, but it has not been observed so far north for many years. It is widespread in Ireland.

The butterfly is creamy-white, and the male (illustrated) has a rather square blackish spot on the tip of the fore wings. In the female the spot is reduced to a few blackish scales. The under sides of the hind wings of many of the spring specimens are dull greenish. Occasionally there is a second brood in the year, the males having smaller and rounder spots, and the females almost none at all.

The egg, which is ribbed, is yellowish-white in colour, and the caterpillars have been known to hatch out about a week after the eggs were laid.

The caterpillar, when full-grown, is of a beautiful green colour, minutely dotted with black in

the front ; dorsal line darker green, edged with
yellowish-green ; spiracular line of a clear yellow,
edged above with darker green. The food-plant
is the Tuberous Pea. Caterpillars from the July
butterflies would feed in August and September.

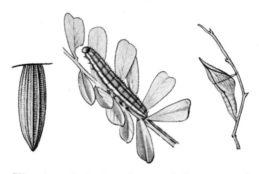

The chrysalis is described as delicate green in
colour, elongated in shape, and tapering slightly
at the ends ; the abdomen rather yellowish, and a
stout pink rib, enclosing the greenish spiracles,
runs all round the body ; from this a strong pink
line branches off, bordering the outer edge of the
wing case, and the nervures of the wings themselves are outlined in pink.

THE BLACK-VEINED WHITE BUTTERFLY

Family PIERIDAE   *Aporia crataegi*

This species has always been uncertain in its appearance in England and about 1925 became extinct in its last known colony in Kent. The butterflies were on the wing at the end of June, and in July. The species is widely distributed on the Continent.

The eggs are upright and ribbed from about the middle, upwards to the ornamental top, which appears as a sort of coronet. The colour is, at first, honey-yellow, then darker yellow, and just before the caterpillar hatches, greyish. They are laid in a cluster on the upper side of a leaf of Sloe, Hawthorn, Plum, etc., in the month of July.

The caterpillar, when full-grown, is tawny-brown with paler hairs arising from white warts; the stripes along the sides and back are black, the under parts are greyish. The head, legs, and spiracles are blackish. Caterpillars hatch from

THE BLACK-VEINED WHITE
BUTTERFLY

the eggs in August, and then live together in a common habitation which is whitish in colour and formed of silk. They come out in the morning, and again in the evening to feed, but a few leaves are generally enclosed in their tenement. In October they seem to retire for the winter and reappear in the spring. During the following May they become full-grown, and then enter the chrysalis state.

The chrysalis is creamy-white, sometimes tinged with greenish, and dotted with black. It is attached by the tail and a girdle of silk.

The butterfly may be recognized by its roundish whitish wings and their conspicuous black veins. On the outer margin of the fore wings there are patches of dusky scales, sometimes absent, forming an irregular dusky border. The female (illustrated) appears slightly darker than the male.

THE LARGE WHITE BUTTERFLY

Family PIERIDAE   *Pieris brassicae*

This familiar butterfly is to be seen annually, in greater or lesser numbers, throughout the British Isles. It is a migratory species, and its varying abundance in any year is dependent chiefly on the arrival of immigrants.

The butterfly is white with rather broad black tips to the fore wings ; there are some black scales along the front margin of these wings. There is a black spot on the front margin of the hind wings in both sexes, but the female (left wing) has, in addition, two roundish black spots on the fore wings, and a black dash from the lower one along the inner margin.

The eggs are yellowish, somewhat skittle-shaped, and prettily ribbed and reticulated. They are laid in batches of from six to over one hundred in each. They are placed on end, and on either side of a leaf, chiefly Cabbage. Caterpillars hatch in about seven days in the summer.

The caterpillar, when full-grown, is greenish.

There are numerous whitish hairs arising from
warts on the back and sides ; the lines are yellow.
They feed in July and again in the autumn on all
plants of the Cabbage tribe, and their presence
is indicated by an evil smell that proceeds from

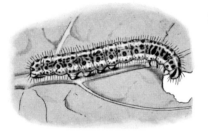

them. A number of these caterpillars may often
be seen crowded together on a cabbage leaf, and
they sometimes abound to such an extent that
much loss is sustained by the cabbage grower.

The chrysalis is grey in colour, more or less
spotted with black and streaked with yellow. It
is fixed horizontally under the top bar of a fence,
or a window-sill; but sometimes in an upright
position when fastened in the angle formed by
two pales. A position protected from the weather
is generally selected.

THE SMALL WHITE BUTTERFLY

Family PIERIDAE   *Pieris rapae*

This species is distributed throughout the British Isles except the Hebrides and Shetlands, and is, perhaps, more often in evidence than the Large White. It is also a migrant, and although it never seems to be absent, in its proper season,

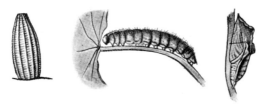

its great increase in numbers in some years is almost certainly due to the arrival of immigrants.

The egg is, at first, pale greenish in colour, but later on it turns yellowish, and this tint is retained until just before the caterpillar hatches out.

The caterpillar, when full-grown, has a brownish head and a green body, sprinkled with black and clothed with blackish hairs emitted from warts. There is a yellowish line on the back, and a line formed of yellow spots on the side. It feeds on most plants of the Cabbage tribe, and in flower gardens on Mignonette and Nasturtiums. It often enters a greenhouse to pupate, and where the house is heated during the winter, the butterfly sometimes emerges quite early in the year.

The chrysalis ranges in tint from pale brown, through grey to greenish ; the markings are black. It is to be found in similar situations to

THE SMALL WHITE BUTTERFLY

those chosen by the Large White, but often under the *lower* rail of a fence or board of a wooden building.

The butterfly, in its spring form, is white, with the tips of the fore wings only slightly clouded with black ; and the black spots in the male (illustrated), near the centre of the wings, are always more or less faint. Sometimes the central spot and the blackish clouding of the tip are absent. The summer brood, on the other hand, has fairly blackish tips and more distinct black spots. In certain favourable years a partial third brood has occurred, but such specimens are often small in size.

THE GREEN-VEINED WHITE
BUTTERFLY

Family PIERIDAE   *Pieris napi*

This butterfly is generally distributed throughout the British Isles, but its range northwards does
not seem to extend beyond Ross. Its favourite
haunts are woods, especially the sunny sides, leafy
lanes, and even marsh land. There are always
two broods in the year, the first on the wing in
May and June, but occasionally as early as April.
The second brood occurs in late July and throughout August.

The butterfly, of which a female specimen of
the summer brood is illustrated, is white with
greenish veins, blackish tips and rounded spots.
There is a tendency for the spots on the fore wings
of the female to spread and run together, forming
an interrupted band. Specimens of a distinct
creamy tint on the wings are sometimes met with.
Seasonal variation is very noticeable in this
species, and much aberration occurs.

The egg is of a pale straw colour when first laid,
but it soon turns to greenish, and as the caterpillar within matures, the shell of the egg becomes

THE GREEN-VEINED WHITE
BUTTERFLY

paler. The ribs are about fourteen in number. The eggs are laid singly on Hedge Garlic, and other kinds of plants belonging to the Wallflower Family.

The caterpillar, when full-grown, is green above with black warts, from which arise whitish and blackish hairs. There is a darker line along the

back, and a yellow line low down on the sides. Underneath the colour is whitish-grey. The spiracular line is dusky, and the spiracles are blackish surrounded with yellow. Caterpillars may be found in June and July, and again in August and September. It has been stated that caterpillars fed upon Hedge Garlic produce lighter coloured butterflies, and those reared on Mignonette and Watercress produce dark butterflies, but confirmation seems to be needed.

The chrysalis is green in colour, and the raised parts are yellowish and brown. This is the most frequent form, but it varies through yellowish to buff or greyish, and is sometimes without markings. It is often attached to stems and branches as well as to palings and walls.

THE BATH WHITE BUTTERFLY

Family PIERIDAE   *Pontia daplidice*

This butterfly is such a rare visitor to this country that anyone seeing a specimen can count himself extremely fortunate. Up to 1945 less than 200 specimens had been recorded. In 1945 an immigration of great magnitude occurred and the species was common and bred freely along the sea-board counties of Southern England.

A specimen was taken even as far north as Lincoln. The immigration also extended to Southern Ireland. Unfortunately, our climate does not seem to be suitable for the species to establish itself here as a permanent resident. The invasion started in mid July, but some of the earlier records note the species in this country in May.

The egg is of a pinkish-red colour, agreeing in size and colour with the anthers of the flowers of Mignonette, upon which plant it is laid in an upright position. It is ribbed and similar in shape to that of an acorn without the cup.

THE BATH WHITE BUTTERFLY

The caterpillar, when full-grown, is bluish-grey, dotted with black warts, from each of which there is a blackish hair. The lines along the back and sides are yellow. Head yellowish, dotted with black, and hairy. It feeds in August and September on garden as well as Wild Mignonette.

The chrysalis is, at first, similar in colour to the caterpillar, but it afterwards becomes whitish. It has numerous black dots, and is marked with yellow along the sides and on the back of the thorax. It is attached by the tail and a silken girdle.

On the upper side of the fore wings the black markings comprise a spot on the fore wings, sometimes divided, and a patch on the tips of the wings ; the latter enclose spots of the ground colour. The markings of the under side show through blackish on the upper side of the hind wings. The female differs from the male in having a black spot between veins 1 and 2 of the fore wings, and the markings of the hind wings are blacker, especially on the outer area.

THE ORANGE-TIP BUTTERFLY

Family PIERIDAE   *Anthocharis cardamines*

This species is generally distributed throughout England, Wales, and Ireland, occurring in Scotland as far north as the Caledonian Canal. The butterfly is on the wing towards the end of May and in June.

The male butterfly (right wing) is white or creamy-white, and has a large patch of orange colour on the outer third of the fore wings, and the extreme tip is blackish. The female is without the orange patch. There are white spots on the outer margin and around the tips of the wings. The hind wings, in both sexes, appear to be dappled with greyish-green, and this is caused by the green marking on the under side showing through. The black spot varies in size and shape, and it is always larger in the male than in the female, and may be entirely absent in the latter sex.

The egg, when first laid, is whitish, faintly tinged with greenish ; it soon changes to yellow, and, later on, turns orange and then dark violet. It is placed upright on the foot-stalks of the flowers of Hedge Mustard or Cuckoo-flower.

THE ORANGE-TIP BUTTERFLY

The caterpillar, when mature, is dull bluish-green, with raised dots and warts ; from the dots arise whitish hairs, and from the warts are blackish hairs. There is a white line along the sides, and the under parts are greener than the

back. The caterpillar, in colour and marking, agrees so closely with the seed-pods of its food-plant that its detection is not always easy. It feeds in June and July.

The chrysalis is curiously elongated, and tapers towards each end ; the back is curved and the wing cases bulge out about the middle of the under side. It is pale grey or whity-brown. The back is speckled with brownish. When the chrysalis is first formed, it is green, and this colour is sometimes retained.

THE BRIMSTONE BUTTERFLY

Family PIERIDAE   *Gonepteryx rhamni*

This butterfly enjoys a longer existence in the perfect state than any of the other British species, with the exception, perhaps, of the Tortoiseshells and their allies. It may be seen any sunny day from March to June in almost every English and Welsh county and locally in I r e l a n d w h e r e its f o o d-plant g r o w s. In the autumn it is often seen flying along t h e outskirts o f woods, and also in Clover fields.

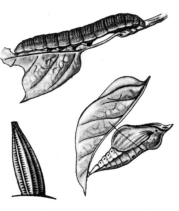

The egg, when first laid, is pale greenish and rather glossy, but it soon changes to yellowish, and later, when the caterpillar is formed inside, to a dull purplish-grey. It is laid on the under side of the leaves of the Buckthorn or of the berry-bearing Alder in May or June. It is usually placed on the rib of a leaf.

The caterpillar, when full-grown, is green, merging into bluish-green on the sides, and thickly powdered with shining black specks. There is a pale line on each side below the spiracles. It feeds in June and July on both kinds of Buckthorn.

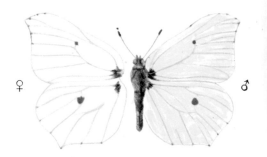

The chrysalis is bluish-green and of a curious shape. The yellowish and brown beak in front, the raised brownish bases of the wing-covers, and the humped thorax, somewhat resemble a bird's head ; also the enlarged wing-cases, which are rather greener than the other parts, give a good imitation of a curled leaf. It is attached by the tail and silken girdle.

The butterfly has the tips of the fore wings sharply pointed, and there is an acute angle about the middle of the outer margin of the hind wings. The colour of the male (right wing) is bright sulphur-yellow, with a central orange spot on each wing. There are also reddish dots on the outer margin of the fore wings, and also along the front margin towards the tip. The female is greenish-yellow, and marked similarly to the male. In both sexes the antennae are reddish, and there is long silky hair on the thorax.

THE SWALLOW-TAIL BUTTERFLY

Family PAPILIONIDAE   *Papilio machaon*

It is curious that, in England, the Swallow-tail is confined mostly to the low-lying fens of Norfolk and Cambridgeshire, whilst on the Continent it is common in woods and meadows, and even on mountains up to 1,500 m (5,000 ft).

This beautiful butterfly, the male of which is illustrated, has yellow wings, ornamented with black, blue, and red. The black markings are chiefly a large patch at the base of the fore wings with a band along the outer portion of all the wings. There are also three black spots on the front margin, and the veins are black. At the lower angle of the hind wings there is a roundish patch of red. The male and female are similar in colour and markings, but the female is larger. The first brood is out at the end of May and early June, and there is a partial second brood at the end of July.

The egg, when first laid, is described as globular in shape, and greenish-yellow, quickly turning to green, and afterwards becoming purplish. It is laid on leaflets of the Milk Parsley in May or June, and again in August.

The caterpillar, when full-grown, is bright green, with an orange-spotted black band on each ring, and blackish marks between the rings. The head is yellow striped with black. After the third change of skin, a remarkable V-shaped fleshy structure of orange colour is developed from a fold of the ring nearest the head. This organ is not always in evidence, but makes its appearance when the caterpillar is annoyed. Other food-plants are Angelica, Fennel, Wild Carrot, etc. From eggs laid in May or June, caterpillars hatch in from ten to twelve days, and these attain the chrysalis state in about six or seven weeks.

Caterpillars from eggs laid in August, may be found in September, and chrysalids from October onwards throughout the winter.

The chrysalis varies in colour from greenish-yellow to brown, and sometimes nearly black. It is most frequently seen on the stems of reeds, on the food-plants, bits of stick, etc.

THE CLOUDED YELLOW BUTTERFLY

Family P*IERIDAE*   *Colias croceus*

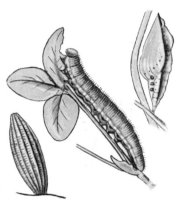

This species has probably occurred in almost every county in England and Wales, Ireland and Scotland. In some of the warmer countries that it inhabits it has three, and possibly four, broods in the year. Some portion of these broods reach our country, proably in the spring of the year. The weather conditions being favourable, the off-spring of the visitors put in an appearance in the autumn.

The butterfly is orange in colour, with broad black borders. Both sexes have a black spot near the centre of the fore wings, and a deep orange spot about the middle of the hind wings. The female (left wing) usually has the black borders spotted with yellow, but in some examples these spots are almost or quite absent. The female is sometimes of a pale yellowish-white colour instead of orange. The males vary from rich orange to the palest yellow ; the marginal bands also vary in width. It should be looked for in Clover or Lucerne fields in August and September.

The eggs are oval, tapering towards each end,

THE CLOUDED YELLOW BUTTERFLY

pale yellow at first, then darker yellow to pink. They are laid on the upper side of a leaf of Clover or Lucerne, sometimes singly, but often in small batches.

The caterpillar, when full-grown, is deep green, with minute black dots with fine hairs, and a pink-marked yellow or whitish spiracular line. The head is also green, rather downy and small in size. It feeds on Clover, Trefoil, Melilot, etc., in June and again in September and October.

The chrysalis is yellowish-green ; the wing-cases are rather deeper in tint than the thorax and back. The body is marked with a splash of reddish and tiny black dots on the under side. The beak-like projection from the head is dark green above and yellow beneath.

THE PALE CLOUDED YELLOW BUTTERFLY

Family PIERIDAE   *Colias hyale*

This usually scarce migrant butterfly has appeared mostly in the Kentish district of England, more or less abundant in some years, quite absent in others and reappearing after long intervals. It seems clear that this species passes the winter as a caterpillar, and it appears equally certain that the caterpillars would not survive an ordinary winter in this country. Possibly, however, in very mild winters, or in certain warm nooks on the south coast, some may be able to exist until the spring, and then complete their growth and reach the butterfly state.

The following particulars of the early stages are adopted from Mr. Frohawk's account of the life-history of the species.

The egg is yellowish-white at first, then through yellow to rosy-orange, and just before the caterpillar hatches out, it changes to a purplish-grey colour.

The caterpillar, when full-grown, is light green, but has a darkish velvety appearance, due to the surface being sprinkled with black warts, from

THE PALE CLOUDED YELLOW
BUTTERFLY

which emerge bristles ; the bristles from the warts on the back are black, and those on the lower surface are white. The line above the spiracles, which are white outlined with black, is made up of yellow, vermilion, and orange with an upper border of white. The head, claspers and legs are green. It feeds in June and August on Clovers, Lucerne, etc.

The chrysalis is very similar to that of the Clouded Yellow, except that the head-beak is straight instead of being slightly upturned, and the tip of the wing-case extends further down the body.

The male butterfly (illustrated) is a primrose-yellow colour ; the female, as a rule, is almost white. The outer margin of the fore wings is black, and there are some more or less united spots of the ground colour towards the tips of the wings. There is a black spot near the middle of the wing. The hind wings have a pale orange central spot, and the narrow blackish border is often broken up into spots. The fringes of all the wings and the antennae are pinkish. When the butterfly occurs in this country it should be looked for in Clover and Lucerne fields in August and September.

BERGER'S CLOUDED YELLOW BUTTERFLY

Family PIERIDAE   *Colias australis*

This butterfly has been found in southern England for many years, but only in 1947 was it proved to be a separate species from the Pale Clouded Yellow.

The butterfly is a migrant, breeding here in favourable years. The size is practically the same as the Pale Clouded Yellow, but the dark border on the hind wings is absent and also less prominent on the fore wings in the new species. The males are a brighter yellow on the upper side and a bright orange on the underside.

The discal spots in both sexes are larger and the females can have either a yellow or white ground colour.

The female lays her eggs on Hippocrepis, and in favourable years there can be two broods.

The winter is passed as a small hibernating larva which rarely, if ever, survives this climate.

The larva differs from that of the Pale Clouded Yellow by having additional sub-dorsal lines and black spots.

The pupa also has pale sub-dorsal lines.

BERGER'S CLOUDED YELLOW BUTTERFLY

THE DINGY SKIPPER BUTTERFLY

Family HESPERIIDAE   *Erynnis tages*

A widely distributed species which should be looked for on open ground, especially in chalky districts.

The butterfly is on the wing in May and June and the female lays her eggs on Bird's-foot Trefoil; the young larva will spend the winter hibernating.

The larva is a yellowish-green with a pale brown head. The chrysalis is made amongst leaves close to the ground.

THE DINGY SKIPPER BUTTERFLY

THE GRIZZLED SKIPPER BUTTERFLY

Family HESPERIIDAE   *Pyrgus malvae*

This butterfly is generally distributed in England and Wales, extending as far north as southern Yorkshire. It is uncommon in Ireland. It is found in May and June on chalk downs and other hillsides, especially in the hollows and sheltered nooks, also in and around woods, and in rough fields. On dull days and at night it may be found sitting, with the wings erect over the back, on various seed-heads, etc. In forward seasons it has been seen on the wing during the last week in April. The species is double-brooded on the Continent, and occasionally a few butterflies will appear in August, but such emergences depend on a combination of favourable circumstances.

The wings of the butterfly are blackish, ornamented with numerous white spots, which are more or less square in shape, on the fore wings. The fringes are chequered black and white.

THE GRIZZLED SKIPPER BUTTERFLY

The male differs from the female (illustrated) in having the front edge of the fore wings folded towards the base. The central series of spots on the hind wings are also more in evidence, and often unite to become bandlike. Variation consists in modification of the markings, chiefly in a tendency of the spots to run together.

The egg is pale green in colour, ribbed, and delicately netted with cross-lines. It is laid on the leaves of Wild Strawberry.

The caterpillar, when full-grown, is whitish-green in colour, and covered with short whitish hair ; a whitish-edged dark brown line along the

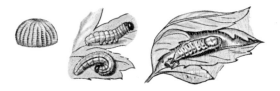

back, and similar lines on the sides ; between the rings the colour is pale ochreous. It feeds on Wild Strawberry and Bramble, and will also eat Raspberry and Cinquefoil. It forms a sort of envelope of a Bramble leaf, spun together with silk, in which the chrysalis is found.

The chrysalis is pale brown, with blackish marks along the back and sides ; the head and back are covered with dense reddish bristles ; the wing, leg, and antennae cases are greenish. Between the head and the first ring of the body above there is a deep furrow, with a black-centred white spot on each side of it.

THE CHEQUERED SKIPPER BUTTERFLY

Family HESPERIIDAE   *Carterocephalus palaemon*

In England this butterfly is found in some of the larger woods of Lincolnshire, Northamptonshire and Buckinghamshire. About 1950 the species was found in quite different terrain near Fort William in Scotland. In its Scottish

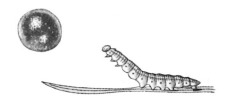

haunts it frequents hillsides with a very sparse growth of trees. Where the species occurs it may be found feeding on flowers of Ground Ivy and Bugle. It is on the wing in June; sometimes it is seen in the latter part of May, and, more rarely perhaps, in July.

The following particulars of the early stages are taken from Mr. Frohawk's life-history of the species :

"The eggs have a pearly appearance, being whitish or yellowish-white in colour, and they were laid on a plant of Brome Grass ; they were laid singly, firmly adhering to the blades of grass. Ten days after the egg is deposited, the young caterpillar emerges by eating away the crown.

"The caterpillar, when one hundred and one days old, was primrose-yellow in colour, with stripes of a darker hue ; there is a white lateral line, and the spiracles are brownish ; the head

THE CHEQUERED SKIPPER BUTTERFLY

pale buff with a black patch above the mouth, and brownish at the sides. About the middle of October the winter shelter is formed by spinning two blades of grass together at the edges, forming a tube, in which the caterpillar remains during the winter.

" The chrysalis is a very pale primrose-yellow, shading into pearly-grey. The head is pointed in front in the form of a beak, and the body gradually tapers to the last segment, terminating in a curved process furnished with long hooks. In general appearance and colouring, the pupa closely resembles a piece of dead withered grass. A female butterfly emerged, from the egg laid in June, about the middle of the following May ; the transformation from egg to perfect insect, therefore, occupied about eleven months."

The butterfly is blackish-brown in the ground colour, and the well-defined yellow or orange spots distinguish this species from all other British Skippers. The variation is only of a minor kind, chiefly in the increase or decrease in the number and the size of the spots. Occasionally those on the fore wings are much enlarged, and the spots on the outer margin of the hind wings are sometimes very small or entirely absent.

THE SMALL SKIPPER BUTTERFLY

Family HESPERIIDAE   *Thymelicus sylvestris*

This butterfly may be found in July and August throughout the greater part of England, south of the Humber and Mersey, and in Wales. It is probably absent from Ireland. Although it does not seem to be very plentiful in the fenlands, it certainly has a partiality for damp places, whether on the sides of woods, on hill slopes, or waste ground. Wherever there is a fairly large growth of the taller soft grasses that the caterpillars feed upon, there the butterfly may be seen.

The butterfly has wings of brownish-orange, with the veins darker, and becoming black towards the outer margins, especially on the fore wings. The male (illustrated) has a black sexual mark. Except that the colour varies in the direction of a pale golden tint, there is little in the way of aberration in this species.

The eggs are described as long ovals, devoid of ribs or reticulation ; at first white, then turning dull yellowish, and at last paler again, with the dark heads of the caterpillars showing through. They are laid in a row in a folded blade of grass.

The caterpillar, when full-grown, is a delicate light green, with a bluish-green stripe along the

THE SMALL SKIPPER BUTTERFLY

back, with pale green central and side lines ; the spiracles are flesh-coloured, and below these there is a creamy-white stripe. The head is deeper green than the body, and roughened with minute points. It feeds in June on various kinds of soft grasses, and its similarity, both in colour and texture, to the blades of grass is remarkable. Before changing to the chrysalis, it encloses itself within two or three leaves of the grass, joined

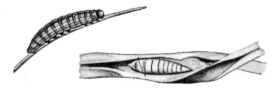

together by lacing with white silk, the edges more or less close to each other, and becomes completely hidden.

The chrysalis is similar in colour to that of the caterpillar, and the lines are fairly in evidence. It is secured in the silken chamber, head upward, by an oblique cincture behind the thorax, and the anal tip fastened by a fan-like spread of fine hooks at the extremity fixed in the silk.

THE ESSEX SKIPPER BUTTERFLY

Family HESPERIIDAE   *Thymelicus lineola*

This species was not acknowledged as British until January 1890, and since that time has been found in a great many parts of Essex, chiefly along the coast, and also in many other southern and eastern counties of England. It is reported as

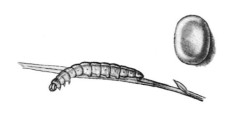

having a partiality for the embankments which protect the cultivated land from the inroad of the high tides which flood the salt marshes. Here it flits about, or rests on the coarse seaside grasses, or on blossoms of Thistle or Bird's-foot Trefoil, indicating rather sluggish habits, yet flying swiftly when disturbed. Further inland it seems to frequent chalky hillsides and marshes. It is on the wing in July and August.

The egg is pale greenish-yellow, oval in shape, flattened above and below ; the top is slightly depressed. The eggs are deposited in July or August, in dried grass seed-heads, and inside the sheaf of a leaf, and the caterpillars are stated not to hatch until April.

The caterpillar is green, with the incisions between the rings yellowish ; there is a darker green stripe on the back, and the lines on the sides

THE ESSEX SKIPPER BUTTERFLY

are yellow. The head is pale brown and striped with darker brown. It feeds from April to June on coarse grasses, such as Couch Grass. When full-grown it spins together the stems of the grass low down, with a network of white silk for pupation.

The chrysalis is described as being long, yellowish-green in colour, and retaining the dark stripe seen in the caterpillar.

The butterfly is very like the Small Skipper, but may be separated from it, in both sexes, by the black under sides of the knobs of the antennae. The black sexual mark in the male is finer, shorter, and much less oblique.

THE LULWORTH SKIPPER BUTTERFLY

Family HESPERIIDAE   *Thymelicus acteon*

This butterfly received its English name as far
back as 1832, when it was first discovered at
Lulworth Cove in Dorsetshire. Its range extends
westward to Devon and Cornwall, and it has been
found in two or three spots along the chalk range
of the Purbeck Hills. It is stated to be only
single brooded, and the best time for it is from the
beginning of July to the middle of August. The
blossoms of Rest-Harrow is said to be the particular vanity of the butterfly, and it is seldom
found visiting any other flower.

The butterfly is dingy brownish in colour, but
it is enlivened, especially in the female by a short
dash and a curved series of orange spots on the
upper half of the fore wings. The male has a
black sexual mark which is very similar to that of
the Small Skipper. There seems to be very little
to note in variation, except that the orange marks
referred to are subject to modification, and in the
male may be altogether absent. An example
taken at Swanage, in 1903, had the wings on the
left side male, and those on the right side,
female.

The egg is whitish, faintly tinged with yellow.

THE LULWORTH SKIPPER BUTTERFLY

The caterpillar, when mature, is pale greyish, or yellowish-green, edged with a slender, pale yellow line on either side, and enclosing a pale longitudinal line along its middle. A narrow yellowish line runs above on the side, and a broader one below. The head is greenish with two yellowish lines. The food-plants of the

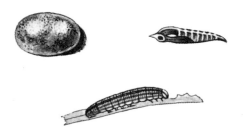

caterpillar are False-Brome and Couch Grasses. It rests in a silk-lined hollow formed by drawing the two edges of a grass blade together with silken strands, afterwards fastening itself within more closely constructed retreats, when it ceases to feed.

The chrysalis is greenish, similar to the colour of the caterpillar, and the lines are faintly traceable.

THE SILVER-SPOTTED SKIPPER BUTTERFLY

Family HESPERIIDAE   *Hesperia comma*

This butterfly is to be found in August on most of our chalk hills, but has not been recorded from either Scotland or Ireland.   It is a very quick flyer, and difficult to capture when on the wing, but it is fond   of sitting on low - growing Thistles, and is then some-what easy to take.

The following details are taken from Mr. Frohawk's account of the life-history of this species :

"The egg, when newly laid, is pearl white, with a slight yellowish-green tinge, which very gradually turns deeper in colour, assuming a pale straw-yellow, and later becoming paler again.   They are laid singly on the fine blades of the Hair Grass. A large number of eggs are finally deposited on the grass-stems and blades.

"The caterpillar, when about one hundred days old, is dull olive-green in colour, with a black collar on the first ring, and the entire surface densely sprinkled with minute shining black warts, emitting a tiny amber-coloured spine with a cleft apex.   The head is blackish marked with ochreous lines.   Directly after leaving the egg, in March or early in April, the caterpillar starts spinning the fine grass together into a dense cluster an inch or so above the ground.   In this shelter it lives and feeds upon the grass surrounding it, remaining almost always completely hidden.

THE SILVER-SPOTTED SKIPPER BUTTERFLY

Just before pupation it spins a coarse network cocoon among the grass close to the ground, and therein pupates during the latter part of July.

" The chrysalis is secured in the cocoon by hooks at the tail, and by hooked bristles on the head; the head and thorax are pale olive, mottled with blackish; the body olive, spotted with darker; below each spiracle, which are amber-brown, is a short longitudinal mark."

The butterfly is very similar on the upper side to the Large Skipper, but the spots, especially those nearest the front edge of the fore wings, are yellower. On the under side the greenish tinge of the ground colour, and the silvery spots, make the identification quite easy. The black sex mark in the male is very similar to that of the Large Skipper.

THE LARGE SKIPPER BUTTERFLY

Family HESPERIIDAE   *Ochlodes venata*

This butterfly is found in most of our English and Welsh counties, and also in Scotland, south of the Forth. It is on the wing from early June until well into July, and sometimes even later in the year, and frequents grassy places on the slopes of downs and other hillsides, also in rides, and on the margins of woods.

The butterfly is tawny yellow, and the male has the discal area of the fore wings bright fulvous, and the outer area broadly brown ; the sexual mark is black. The hind wings are tinged with fulvous on the disc, and have brighter fulvous spots. The female generally is brown with a fulvous discal wedge on the fore wings and a series of spots, of similar colour, beyond ; hind wings as in the male, but spots rather more defined. In some examples of this sex the spots on the fore wings are confluent, and the discal area is then fulvous, as in the male. The egg-laying of this species has been observed, and shows that the butterfly alights on a blade of grass almost parallel to its longer axis. It then curves its abdomen round beneath the blade and deposits an egg almost in the centre of the blade.

The egg is whitish or greenish-white.

THE LARGE SKIPPER BUTTERFLY

The caterpillar, it is stated, emerges from the egg in about twelve days after the egg is laid early in July, and chooses Cock's-foot Grass for food ; resting in the middle of a blade, and  fastening its edges across with five or six little ropes of white silk. After hibernation, in the following May, it is about one inch long, and pale green in colour; the skin is thickly covered with very short dark brown bristles ; the head is dirty white, with a dark brown stripe down the outer edge of each lobe, the neck being whitish-green.

The chrysalis, in general colour, is brown, with the wing cases darker, and a dark suffusion on the back. It is placed in a cocoon among grass.

INDEX